Milita[illegible] and Kashmir

Luv Puri ha[illegible] ammu and Kashn[illegible] id has reported fr[illegible] i is the recipient of several [illegible] ling the European Commission Award for Human Rights and Democracy.

Militancy in Jammmu and Kashmir

The Uncovered Face

Luv Puri

PROMILLA & CO., PUBLISHERS
in association with
BIBLIOPHILE SOUTH ASIA

NEW DELHI & CHICAGO

Published by
PROMILLA & CO., PUBLISHERS
in association with
BIBLIOPHILE SOUTH ASIA
URL : www.biblioasia.com

C-127, Sarvodaya Enclave
New Delhi 110 017, India

First published 2008

ISBN : 978-81-85002-90-3

Typeset in Times New Roman
Layout and processing by Radius Arc, New Delhi

Printed and bound in India by
Bibliophile South Asia (Printing Division), New Delhi

Contents

Acknowledegments 7

Introduction 9

1. Jammu: A Link Between the Kashmir Valley and the Rest of India 13

2. The Outbreak of Militancy 24

3. Initiation of Militancy in the Border Districts 39

4. Highway Routes 62

5. Militancy Strikes the Winter Capital 77

6. Conclusion 89

Bibliography 112

Index 114

List of Photographs

1. Lashkar militant eliminated in a combined operation of J&K Police and VDC personnel in Doda district in 2007 38
2. Mariam Begum who was abducted by militants in 2004 in Doda district, with her ears and nose chopped off 38
3. Indian Troops patrolling along the LoC in Poonch district 41
4. Members of the Gujjar tribe 45
5. Village Defence Committee in Rajouri district 55
6. Locally recruited Special Police Officers undergoing training 55
7. A nine-year-old child who was forcibly recruited by militants, demonstrating his skills in using automatic weapons 68
8. Local women of Reasi district learn to use .303 rifle 71
9. Local men of Reasi district learn to use .303 rifle 71
10. A Gujjar Muslim girl injured in a militant attack 72
11. Local Gujjar men fight against militancy in Poonch district 93
12. Surrender ceremony of militants 94
13. Relatives gather on either side of LoC after opening of LoC points 95
14. A view of Pakistani troops along the LoC adjoining Poonch district 95
15. Pakistan-administered Jammu and Kashmir residents being tear-gassed 96
16. Punjabi-speaking Mohammad Shahzad, District Commander Lashkar-e-Toeba, a militant apprehended by Indian troops 100

List of Maps

1. Map of Doda district 28
2. Map of Kishtwar district 28
3. Map of Ramban district 29
4. Map of Poonch district 40
5. Map of Rajouri district 40
6. Reasi district (Before 2006, Reasi was part of Udhampur district) 63
7. Map of Udhampur district 63
8. Map of Kathua district 73
9. Map of Jammu tehsil 79
10. Samba district (Before 2006, Samba was part of Jammu district) 79

Acknowledgements

This study was undertaken through the sponsorship of the Prem Bhatia Memorial Trust. Its Managing Trustee, Shakuntala Bhatia, felt strongly that this work be published, so that scholars and the general public, interested in conflict areas like Jammu and Kashmir, would be benefited. This monograph owes a debt to my illustrious father, Balraj Puri, an acknowledged authority on Jammu and Kashmir. He put me in touch with his lifelong contacts in diverse parts of the state and helped me formulate an overall perspective of the work. I wish to express my gratitude to my sister, for equipping me with the academic and theoretical tools to deal with the subject, and to my mother, for her much-needed encouragement.

Special thanks are due to my Editor-in-Chief N. Ram and Resident Editor Harish Khare who have encouraged me to report on unexplored areas of the state of Jammu and Kashmir. My publisher, Ashok Butani, deserves a special word of appreciation for his professionalism and accommodating attitude, which makes an author's task so much easier. I thank Sherna Wadia for her editing contribution; Tarun Beri, for formatting the text and placing the photographs in their rightful places; Netra Shyam, for her cover design; B.D. Diwan, for proofreading; and Dr. S. S. Bloeria for making available the latest maps of the districts of Jammu and Kashmir.

Acknowledgements

Introduction

This book seeks to contribute to the large corpus of studies on militancy in the Indian administered Jammu and Kashmir (J&K).[1] It focuses attention on largely neglected regional and ethnic aspects of militancy. It traces the origin and growth of militancy to the south of the Pir Panjal range which divides the Kashmir valley and Jammu region.[2] Besides contributing to the debate on the complex issues of Jammu and Kashmir, the book tries to introduce a fresh perspective on the discourse on terrorism through extensive field work. The ethnic and religious diversities that exist in the state of Jammu and Kashmir, particularly to the south of the Pir Panjal, and their impact in shaping the course of militancy in the area, form the core of the study.

The work relies on several years of work by the author in the conflict-ridden parts of the state. Due to the inaccessibility of the region and the complexities of the issues, there is hardly any material available about militancy in this area. Much has been written on militancy in Kashmir but there is hardly any mention about militancy in Jammu. The fact that civilian killings in Jammu constitute 35 % of the total killings in Jammu and Kashmir between 1989 and 2007 has not been taken note of by most observers.[3] The study of militancy in Jammu, therefore, has greater relevance in formulating effective counter-terror strategies in several areas across the world. Further, on the scale of intensity, these killings have been far more brutal in Jammu as compared to the Kashmir valley. For a scholar, militancy in the multi-ethnic and multi-religious Jammu region offers new lessons, which may not be present in a homogenous entity like the Kashmir valley. For instance, heterogeneity of the Muslim community in this region and its differing impact on how militancy has expressed itself could help scholars studying the relationship between religious diversities and militant movements in conflict ridden areas like Jammu and Kashmir.

This study throws up some interesting results, which reinforce the point that the war against terrorism cannot be treated merely as a military problem but has to involve an understanding of the political and societal landscape of a society in turmoil. The time covered in this book is from mid 1990s to 2003, though years preceding as well as following are also looked at. 2003 is taken as a cut-off date because militancy abated considerably in this area from then. The threat has reduced but not fully abated as by the mid-2008, 300 to 400 militants were still active in the region and fresh infiltration attempts continue.[4] The study underscores the need for a long-term solution to the problem to make sure it does not recur.

Jammu's Diversity and Militancy

In sharp contrast to the Kashmir valley, Jammu is more diverse in several ways. The impact of militancy in a mixed society would obviously be different from that in a homogenous one. The causes of the origin and the various stages of the growth of militancy in Jammu, which is situated south of the mighty Pir Panjal, were different from those in Kashmir. It started much later in Jammu. The character, composition and the objectives of militancy in the two regions also varied. The distinctive character of militancy in the two regions is a result of special features such as geography, ethno-religious composition and the socio-political situation. Thus, as long as militancy comprised of the youth from the Kashmir valley and was inspired by the ideology of Kashmiri nationalism, it did not have much appeal in the ethnically different region of Jammu. But when the youth from Pakistan-administered Jammu and Kashmir and the province of Punjab in Pakistan joined the militant movement, it changed from a Kashmiri to a Muslim movement. The response to this in Kashmir was a decline in its appeal, but in Jammu, which was ethnically closer to the new militants, the appeal increased.

The Hindu backlash against the mass killings of innocents, which was a special feature of militancy in Jammu, as also the lapses and excesses of the security forces in areas removed from the gaze of the media and Human Rights activists, further contributed to a vicious cycle of distrust. As Jammu had a smaller share in political power, which was concentrated in the hands of the Kashmiri leadership, the ensuing frustrations often resulted in a communal outlet, which fed the militant movement. The ignorance of the political leadership of the state and the country, and of the planners of security strategies about the peculiarities of the region, further handicapped counter-militancy measures. These and allied problems are covered in this study, which also takes note of the diversities within the region. An areawise analysis of the situation is added to that of the overall trends in the region.

As this is the first study of its kind, it cannot claim to be perfect. But it is hoped that the material and ideas provided by the study will generate sufficient interest for scholars to undertake more in-depth studies into this vital aspect of the Jammu and Kashmir problem, which poses one of the greatest challenges to India. In this work I have used the word militant to identify non-state actors who use violent means to achieve political goals. The term militant is used as opposed to terrorist, because it is used in common parlance in Jammu and Kashmir. The word insurgency has been used to define the phase in the state when mass-scale people's support existed particularly in Kashmir valley and Doda district of Jammu region for separation from India. This phase was marked by large scale demonstrations participated by common people in early 1990s.

Notes

1. The state of Jammu and Kashmir on the Indian side comprises three distinct ethnic and geographical regions namely Jammu, Kashmir valley and Ladakh. Both Jammu region and Kashmir valley have been affected by militancy whereas Ladakh has remained peaceful. Most of the studies have been done on Kashmir valley and wrongly termed as work on the entire state. This has largely ignored the autonomous factors which have underpinned the conflict in Jammu region. The state of J&K as it existed before 1947 is presently divided into Indian-administered J&K and Pakistan-administered Jammu and Kashmir. The two are divided by approx.740 km Line of Control.
2. Pir Panjal is the mountain range of the Himalayas that divides the Kashmir valley and the Jammu region. Pir Panjal is not only a geographical barrier between the two regions, it is also an ethnic and cultural divide.
3. This information was given by the J&K Chief Minister, Ghulam Nabi Azad, in the January 2008 budget session of the J&K Legislative Assembly.
4. Lt-Gen R.K. Karwal, General Officer in Command of Nagrota-based 16 Corps of the Army made this disclosure to media-persons on 9th April, 2008.

1

Jammu: A Link Between the Kashmir Valley and the Rest of India

Jammu is the primary geo-political link between the Kashmir valley and the rest of India. Developments in the Jammu region have often affected the situation in Kashmir and vice versa. However, there are autonomous causes for developments in each region. This fact has often been ignored by studies on the Kashmir problem, in particular, of the militancy in the state. Though it had its origin in Kashmir, militancy reached different parts of Jammu at different times. It was in no sense an automatic extension of the Kashmiri insurgency. Local causes contributed to it. Even the timings of the emergence of militancy in different parts of the region differed. No study of militancy in any part of state would be complete, nor could an effective counter-militancy policy be evolved, without studying social and political history of the state, that is, both Jammu and Kashmir valley.

Pre-Partition Profile of Jammu and Kashmir

The present state of Jammu and Kashmir comprises three distinct regions – Jammu, Kashmir and Ladakh. Before 1947, the territorial boundaries of the state were different. As per 1931 census, J&K with an area of 2,18,780 sq kms approximately, was the largest of the 565 princely states of India. Jammu province occupied an area of 32,067 sq kms, Kashmir province, 22,165 sq kms, and the frontier district of Ladakh and Gilgit, 1,64,604.86 sq kms. Jammu province was divided into six districts, namely Udhampur (including the present day Doda district), Reasi, Mirpur, Poonch, Jammu and Kathua. Kashmir region comprised of four districts – Srinagar, Baramulla, Anantnag and the non-Kashmiri-speaking Muzaffarabad. Third region was Ladakh and Gilgit. With the marking of the Ceasefire Line between India and Pakistan in Jammu and Kashmir on January 1, 1949, the area of the state under India's control was effectively reduced to 1,38,992 sq kms. The impact of this division on the state was enormous in general and in particular on Jammu's social and political history.

In terms of area, Jammu province was reduced to 26,689.4 sq kms, and Kashmir to 15,520 sq kms. The population of Jammu region, according to the census report of 1941, was 19,81,433, whereas that of Kashmir was 17,28,705, and the districts of Ladakh and Gilgit 3,11,478 people. Besides an obvious territorial change resulting from this division, the demographic profile was also altered. A Muslim majority Jammu now became Hindu majority, primarily because the Mirpur district and parts of Poonch jagir, which had Muslim majority now became part of Pakistan-administered Jammu and Kashmir. The density of population in Poonch jagir with 172 persons per sq km followed by Mirpur (159) was one of the highest in the state. In the areas of Jammu province that went to Pakistan, Muslim Rajputs, Suddhans, Gujjars and Jats constituted a considerable chunk. The total number of Muslim Rajputs was 2,26,000, and their strongholds were the Mirpur district and the Poonch jagir. Muslim Jats lived in the western part of Jammu province and their number was 1,21,000 with the majority living in Mirpur. Gujjars, a nomadic community spread across the hilly parts of Jammu province had a population of 2,72,431 people at the time of the division of the state. Even after the division, the Gujjar population in Jammu province constitutes a sizeable number, despite migration from the peripheral areas of Jammu district to Pakistan and Pakistan-administered Jammu and Kashmir. These details become particularly relevant in understanding the unfolding of events in Jammu with regard to the growth of militancy in the last two decades. Clearly, going by the figures, Jammu province was the most seriously affected by communal riots during the Partition. The events of 1947 caused large-scale movement of people. The migration of Muslims from the Hindu-dominated parts of Jammu and inflow of Hindus from Pakistan-administered Jammu and Kashmir to the Indian side of the state took place amidst massive communal frenzy.

In 1947, according to figures of J&K government as many as 31,619 families migrated from Pakistan-administered Jammu and Kashmir, which was before 1947 administratively part of Jammu region except non-Kashmiri speaking Muzaffarabad district which was part of Kashmir province. Of these, 26,319 came to J&K while the rest migrated to other parts of India. Most of the migration from the Indian side of J&K took place from Jammu plains. Majority of the migrants went to Sialkot district of Punjab province of Pakistan as it was geographically near to Jammu plains as compared to Pakistan-administered Jammu and Kashmir. Pakistan authorities reported that by 22nd October 1947, at least 100,000 Muslim refugees from Jammu were present in the neighbourhood of Sialkot area of Pakistan.[1] Therefore, displacement on either side of the Line of Control within the state principally in Jammu region, was not less than 2,50,000.

The Socio-Political Scene at the Close of 1947

The Political Scenario

The political movement that started in the Kashmir valley in 1931 under the leadership of Kashmiri leader Sheikh Abdullah did not find a constituency in Jammu even though latter was a Muslim majority region, partly because of the movement's anti-Dogra character. The political divide between Jammu and Kashmir became as wide as the cultural and geographical divide between them. In fact, Sheikh Abdullah's comrades in Jammu left him one by one. Chowdhary Ghulam Abbas was the first to leave the National Conference, not long after it was formed. Among the Muslim leaders, Chowdhary Mohammad Shaffee under the Congress banner was able to extend an effective political base, mainly among the Hindus of Jammu. However, the Congress Party gave its unflinching support to the Sheikh and recognized only his party, the National Conference as the representative of Jammu and Kashmir. With such a lack of secular parties, the Muslim Conference, which was accepted by the Muslim League as its representative, emerged as the vocal voice of the community, while the Hindu Sabha sought to fill the vacuum in the Hindu community. The political soil of Jammu was thus fertile for the communal riots in 1947.

Surgical Operation

Partition of the state in 1947, struck a serious blow to Jammu's personality. It was the most populous region of the state before independence. The Ceasefire Line of 1949 – later re-named the Line of Actual Control after the Indo-Pakistan war of 1971 cut off a major portion of Jammu region, while the Kashmir valley remained more or less intact. Large-scale communal bloodshed and transfer of Hindu and Muslim populations across the Ceasefire Line caused not only untold suffering to the people, but also distorted Jammu's secular character. The problem of rehabilitating hundreds of thousands of Hindu and Sikh refugees displaced from Pakistan-administered Jammu and Kashmir and settled in different parts of the state, still lingers even after six decades of independence, causing several tensions in the region. The Ceasefire Line changed Jammu's Muslim majority into a minority while most of the Muslim leadership of the region migrated or was deported by the state government to Pakistan during those troubled days.

The Social Scenario in the Rajouri-Poonch and Present Day Pakisatn-administered Jammu and Kashmir

Areas of Rajouri-Poonch and present day Pakistan-administered Jammu and Kashmir had Muslim majority; Muslim Rajputs, Jats and Suddhans were an influential group before 1947. They had fought several battles under the Dogra rulers to build up the state. In terms of percentage of population, they provided the largest recruitment in the country to the British army in the Second World War. For instance, Bagh tehsil in Poonch district was almost totally dependant on employment in the army to earn a livelihood. Due to the influence of neighbouring Punjab which was affected by communal violence and the internal politics of the state they rebelled against Maharaja with the active support from Pakistan leading to the creation of Pakistan-administered Jammu and Kashmir.

The Aftermath of the Indo-Pakistan Wars of 1965 and 1971

Jammu was also the worst sufferer in the Indo-Pakistan wars of 1965 and 1971. Of the 315 sq kms of Indian territory invaded by the Pakistani forces in 1965, roughly 285 sq kms were in the Chhamb sector of Jammu.[2]

> The thrust of the raiders too, was deepest in the region beyond 100 miles, on the south of the Pir Panjal range. Again, out of a total displaced population of 2,70,000, as many as 2,50,000 belonged to Jammu. The latter estimate was subsequently revised to 3,00,000. If we include Muslim refugees who fled in the opposite direction, the number would be colossal, affecting at least every fourth household in the region. Apart from problems bequeathed to the region by war and politics, natural factors also contributed to a lack of unity and stability. Unlike other regions of the state, Jammu abounds in geographical, cultural, linguistic, communal, caste and class diversities. Bounded by the river Ravi and the Pir Panjal range, its altitude varies from almost sea-level to 16,000 feet. The rise is so steep, that while the city of Jammu, the winter capital of the state, on occasion records the highest temperature in the country, the snowline is just about 45 kilometres away. In terms of the number of religious communities living in the region, the languages and dialects spoken by its people, the diversity is equally pronounced.[3]

According to the census of 1981, the population of the region was 27 lakhs, which was 45 per cent of the total population of the state and lived in an area of a little over 26,000 sq kms. Hindus constituted 62 per cent of the region's population while 33.8 per cent were Muslims. The population of the Jammu region according to the 2001 Census is 44,30,191 which is 43.67 percent of the state's population. The other communities of Jammu include Sikhs, Christians, Jains and Buddhists. Jammu, after the Partition, has less population than the Kashmir valley but constitutes a larger area. The population in the Kashmir valley outnumbers that of Jammu by about 10.46 lakhs. The differences in the figures of the 1981 and 2001 censuses can be explained mainly by the fact that the army men posted in the region after the outbreak of militancy in Kashmir region were also counted in the figures of Kashmir. The single largest linguistic community in Jammu is that of the Dogras. Dogri is the mother tongue of about 54 per cent of the population. Other principal languages in the region are Gojri, Pahari and Punjabi, apart from several dialects spoken by a smaller number of people, including Bhaderwahi, Poonchi, Siraji, Kisthwari, Pothwari, Padari and Pogli.

Kashmir Valley's Set-up: From Accession to Alienation

Unlike Jammu, Partition did not disturb the ethnic base of Kashmiri speaking population as Kashmir valley remained a single entity .The decision of Maharaja Hari Singh, the ruler of Jammu and Kashmir, to accede to the Indian Union on October 26, 1947 had overwhelming popular support of Kashmir valley. The premier political party of the valley, the National Conference, and its most charismatic leader, Sheikh Abdullah, endorsed it. However, accession came to be questioned by the same people who had supported it in 1947 because of growing differences between the centre and state as well as the changing regional equations within J&K between Kashmir valley and Jammu. A number of national and international factors complicated the situation, resulting in Sheikh Abdullah's dismissal from power and arrest on August 9, 1953.[4]

The consequent alienation of Kashmiri Muslims assumed several forms. Kashmir's freedom movement which itself had a close affinity with, and support of the Indian national movement, in particular its leaders, like Gandhi, Nehru, Azad and Abdul Ghaffar Khan. In fact, during his long incarceration and political isolation from Indian national sentiments, the Sheikh retained the sympathy and support of leaders like Jayaprakash Narayan and C. Rajagopalachari and the Socialist Party. Thus, the division of Pakistan and the emergence of Bangladesh in 1971 provided a fresh opportunity for a dialogue between Sheikh Abdullah and the Government of India, which culminated in his return to power in 1975. The Centre agreed to review the laws extended to the state after his arrest in 1953, on the recommendation of the state government, while Sheikh Abdullah promised to concede regional autonomy to satisfy the regional aspirations of Jammu and Ladakh.

The Start of Militancy in Kashmir Valley

The relationship between the Kashmir valley and the Indian union has witnessed many ups and down right from the state's accession on October 26, 1947. From 1953 to 1971, the Plebiscite Front led by Sheikh Abdullah was the dominant force in Kashmir valley. From the 1970s to the mid-80s the situation in the Kashmir valley was about as normal as any other part of the country. In 1984, duly elected government led by Farooq Abdullah, son of Sheikh Abdullah was dismissed by Central government by engineering defections from his party. Two years later, Farooq patched up with the then Congress Party after agreeing to share power with it, much to the annoyance of his Kashmir-based following. Rajiv Gandhi, the Congress Prime Minister at the time, in a later interview with an Indian journalist termed it the biggest blunder of his life.[5] This coalition also closed the secular outlet for popular discontent, as it left very little space for an opposition in the Kashmir valley. This outlet was further closed by the massive rigging of the March 1987 assembly elections since it also meant a disappearance of the democratic space where this discontent could be expressed. The main nucleus of the militancy movement that followed was formed by the people who had fought the elections, but were fraudulently declared defeated, arrested and humiliated.[6] Many in sheer frustration crossed over to Pakistan and got training and arms to start a violent liberation movement in the state. They established contacts with, and became part of, the Jammu and Kashmir Liberation Front (JKLF) led by the Pakistan-based Amanullah Khan.[7] JKLF made its presence felt by powerful bomb blasts in Srinagar and an abortive attempt on the life of the DIG Police at his residence on September 17, 1989. In January 1990, the state came under President's rule and the Governor dissolved the State Assembly. Hence one other check on the executive power, which keeps the democratic polity alive, was removed from the state.

The ruthless manner in which the militant activities were sought to be suppressed turned it into an insurgency. The founder of the JKLF, Amanullah Khan, led a historic march on February 11, 1992, as a symbolic violation of the Line of Control (LoC) that divides the state of Jammu and Kashmir between India and Pakistan. The JKLF cadre was attacked and 21 people were killed by the Pakistani security forces. The initial phase of militancy, which was dominated by the JKLF cadre gave way to a movement led by pro-Jamat-e-Islami, Hizbul Mujahideen (HM). HM, with the support of the Pakistan government, eclipsed the JKLF. Several members of the JKLF were eliminated in encounters by security forces. The JKLF blamed the HM, which was trying to push it into the background. The JKLF Chief, Amanullah Khan, said, 'It was an attempt by Pakistan to hijack the movement and of vested interests to communalize it.'[8] Later, the militant movement witnessed the emergence of new groups like the Lashkar-e-Toiba and lately the Jaish-e-Muhammad, which, by its more sensational acts, overshadowed even the HM.[9]

Militancy in the Jammu Region

The militancy in the Jammu region, the other half of the state, followed a completely different pattern from that of the Kashmir valley. During the initial three years, the entire province was untouched by the Kashmir insurgency. The region comprises ten districts – Doda, Kishtwar, Ramban, Reasi, Samba, Udhampur, Kathua, Jammu, Rajouri and Poonch.[10] Kishtwar, Ramban, Reasi and Samba are new districts, which were created in 2006 by the Congress-led J&K government. Prior to that, Kishtwar and Ramban were part of Doda district; Reasi was part of Udhampur district; and Samba part of Jammu district. Much of this study was carried out before the creation of the new districts in 2006, therefore the administrative divisions existing before 2006 have been taken as reference points.

The first major act of militancy in the Jammu region occurred in Doda district in 1993. It later spread to other parts of the region. Doda was also the first district where mass-scale killings of the minority community occurred. The twin border districts of Rajouri and Poonch, situated on the sensitive LoC, remained untouched by militancy during the first five years of its emergence in the valley. But militants who were infiltrating from this part to the Kashmir valley soon started setting up their bases here and carrying out active operations. It was realized that tackling militancy in this hilly belt was a most challenging task for the security personnel, due to several factors. Militancy in the province reached its peak with sensational acts in the heart of Jammu city, like the attack on the Raghunath Mandir. Also, in the peripheral areas of the city, there were gruesome terrorists attacks of an unprecedented nature, such as the ones in Rajiv Nagar and Kaluchak, in which at least 60 people including women and children were killed.

Notes

1. Lamb Alastair, *Incomplete Partition* (Roxford 1997), p.128.
2. Interview with Balraj Puri, expert on Jammu and Kashmir studies.
3. Puri, Balraj, *Simmering Volcano: Jammu's Relations with Kashmir*

(Sterling: New Delhi, 1983), p. 3. The state of Jammu and Kashmir acceded to the Indian Union on October 26, 1947. Prior to 1947 it was a princely state with British sovereignty over it.

4. Sheikh Abdullah, the Prime Minister of Jammu and Kashmir was arrested on charges of conspiracy against the state on August 9, 1953. Ghulam Mohammad Bakshi, a former lieutenant of Sheikh Abdullah, was made the Prime Minister.
5. Vir Saghvi referred to this conversation with Rajiv Gandhi in his Sunday column in *The Hindustan Times*, October 2006.
6. The Muslim United Front was an amalgam of political parties fighting the 1987 assembly elections. Mohammad Yosuf Shah, better known as Syed Salahuddin, head of the Hizbul Mujahideen and now living in Pakistan, had also contested the elections from the Amirakadal assembly constituency of Srinagar city. His rival from the National Conference and the former J&K Minister, Ghulam Mohiuddin Shah, defeated him in the election, which was largely believed to be rigged.
7. Amanullah Khan was born in the Gilgit area in the north, which was part of the state of Jammu and Kashmir. He believes in an independent, secular and federal state of Jammu and Kashmir.
8. Interview of Amanullah Khan with the author at his Rawalpindi office, January 2006.
9. Ibid.
10. In July 2006, the J&K cabinet under the chairmanship of Chief Minister Ghulam Nabi Azad decided that four more districts in the Kashmir valley and Jammu region would be carved out of the existing ones. Subsequently the total number of districts in both regions increased to ten each from the earlier six each.

2

The Outbreak of Militancy

The eruption of militancy in the Jammu region happened in spurts. In the early 1990s, when militancy engulfed the Kashmir valley, all the ten districts of Jammu region were peaceful.[1] Security experts could not explain this fact. But what surprised them more was that when they least expected militancy to gain ground in Jammu region, it did. Various reasons have been given for this phenomenon. One popular explanation is that the militants sought refuge in Jammu region when they came under pressure from the security forces in the Valley. Even though in the early nineties, the Rajouri and Poonch areas provided the main infiltration routes for the Kashmiri-speaking militants to sneak into Indian territory, they found difficult to carry out active operations there, and get local response. This was in sharp contrast to the 1947 and 1965 wars between India and Pakistan.

In 1947 or even in 1965, the Pakistani forces were able to capture several areas due to the local support of the people. The invaders and infiltrators in 1947 and 1965 respectively, largely belonged to the same ethnic stock as that of the people in these districts, whereas they were not able to get any response from the Kashmiri-speaking population in the Kashmir valley. In fact, the people of the valley helped the Indian army by working in many places as its informers.

In his book titled *Kashmir and the 1965 War*, Mirpur born Shabir Chowdhary says that the "mujahideen" who were sent to "liberate Kashmir" were from "Azad Kashmir" and they did not know Kashmiri language and traditions.[2] They looked different from the people of the valley and were not aware of the climatic, geographical and social fabrics of Kashmir. These very contradictions in the attitudes of both regions were manifested when the Kashmiri insurgency started in 1989, when it failed to inspire the Muslims of Rajouri and Poonch for a considerable length of time.The first area in Jammu region where militancy made its presence felt in the early nineties was Doda district, which can be considered as a 'cultural bridge' between Kashmir region and Jammu region. The events in Doda shook the security apparatus, since it has a large and mountainous terrain, the security grid could not respond immediately. The arc of militancy in the mid nineties also engulfed the hills of Reasi in the areas of Gool, Gulabgarh and Mahore, where the Muslim community lives in sizeable numbers.

Strangely, the border belt of Rajouri and Poonch, both Muslim-dominated districts were affected by militancy as late as 1995. It was after the 1996 J&K assembly elections that militancy took root in these two districts. A section of Gujjars, an ethnic group (who are 100 per cent Muslim in the state) also started wavering from their broad pro-India line and joined the ranks of the militants. Later, the militants were also able to recruit people from certain parts of Kathua. The militancy in the state, which in the early nineties was a Kashmiri revolt, acquired an Islamic character when it hit the Muslim parts of Jammu region. By 1995, militancy outgrew its Kashmiri character. In sharp contrast to the Kashmir valley, militancy in Jammu was pioneered by pro-Pakistani militants and Islamic groups like the Harkat-ul-Ansar, Hizbul Mujahideen and Muslim Janbaaz. The character of militancy here was distinctively different from that in Kashmir. In Kashmir the first mass killings of Hindus, that is the Kashmiri Pandit community, occurred at Wandhama as late as January 1998, whereas the first mass communal killing in the Doda district of Jammu region was in 1993. The religiously diverse society of Jammu region was bound to be disturbed by the Islamic nature of the militancy hitting it.

Militancy reached its climax in the region by 2001, when it struck in the heart of Jammu city and its suburbs where Hindus were the victims. It hit the headlines in the media with one sensational militant strike after another. The terrain and diversity, discussed earlier, give us a broad sketch of the region. The militants struck at will with the larger design of provoking a religious conflict by targeting temples. Most of the attackers in all these sensational and brutal militant strikes belonged to the non-Kashmiri speaking stock of militants who had come across the approximately 198-kilometre-long Indo-Pak international border along the Jammu frontier.

Any study on militancy in the region, therefore, has to examine the geographic, ethnic and cultural factors, which were and still are, equally responsible for its spread. Although it is difficult to show a definite process of growth of militancy in the region, an examination of local and other factors may shed some light. In order to do so, there is a need to examine the local environment in which the militants operated in different areas of Jammu region.

Geo-Ethnic Variations in Jammu and Its Effects on Militancy

The militancy that at one time engulfed the entire Jammu region did not start at once in all its ten districts. Militancy also threatened Jammu's security, identity and peace with the complementary triple phenomena of militancy, communalism and criminalization. Indeed no effective long-term security policy in the country can be formulated by ignoring the Jammu factor.

Initiation of Militancy in Jammu Region: Doda

Doda was the first district in Jammu region where militancy struck root. But this happened only after it had gained ground in all the districts of the Kashmir valley. In August 1991, a bomb exploded at the district headquarters, which surprised many. The blast was not aimed at causing any damage but was a symbolic demonstration of the presence of the militants. The pioneer insurgent groups were the Muslim Janbaaz and the Hizbul Mujahideen. Strikingly, both groups stood for the state's accession to Pakistan. This was in contrast to Kashmir, where the militant movement was initiated by the JKLF for Kashmir's independence, representing Kashmiri nationalism.

As internal communication infrastructure in the Doda district is still in its infancy, the people in one area had little idea of what was happening in another. But broadly speaking, the youth who joined the militant ranks from the district were from middle-class homes. Among the youth who picked up the gun, there was also a section that had studied in Jammu and returned to Doda.

Sociological Reasons for the Rise of Militancy in Doda

Doda district is a melting pot of many cultures. There are as many as 12 languages and dialects spoken. But broadly speaking, it is the confluence of Kashmiri and Dogra cultures. Dialects change within a range of a few kilometres. For instance, while in Doda town Kashmiri is spoken, in the surrounding area, that is in its

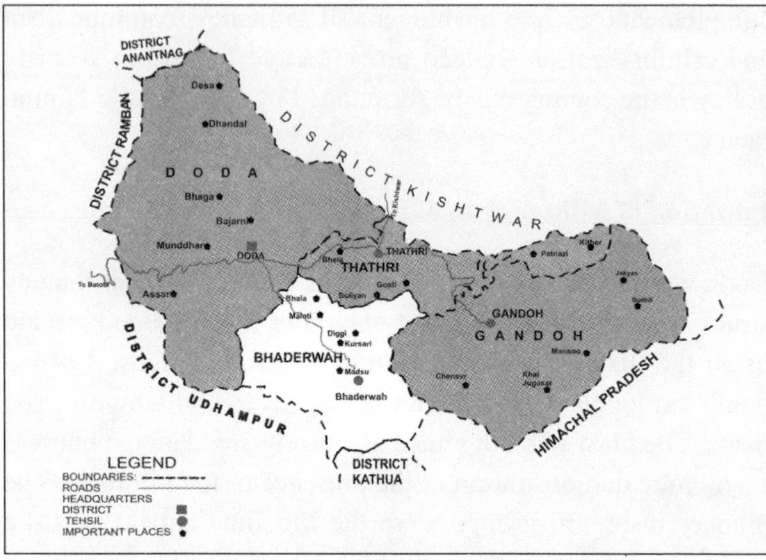

Map of Doda district

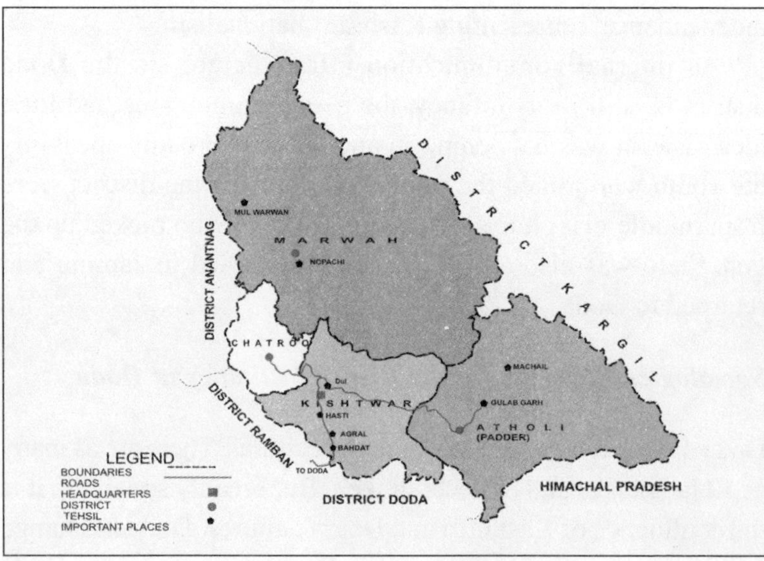

Map of Kishtwar district
(Before 2006, Kishtwar was part of Doda district)

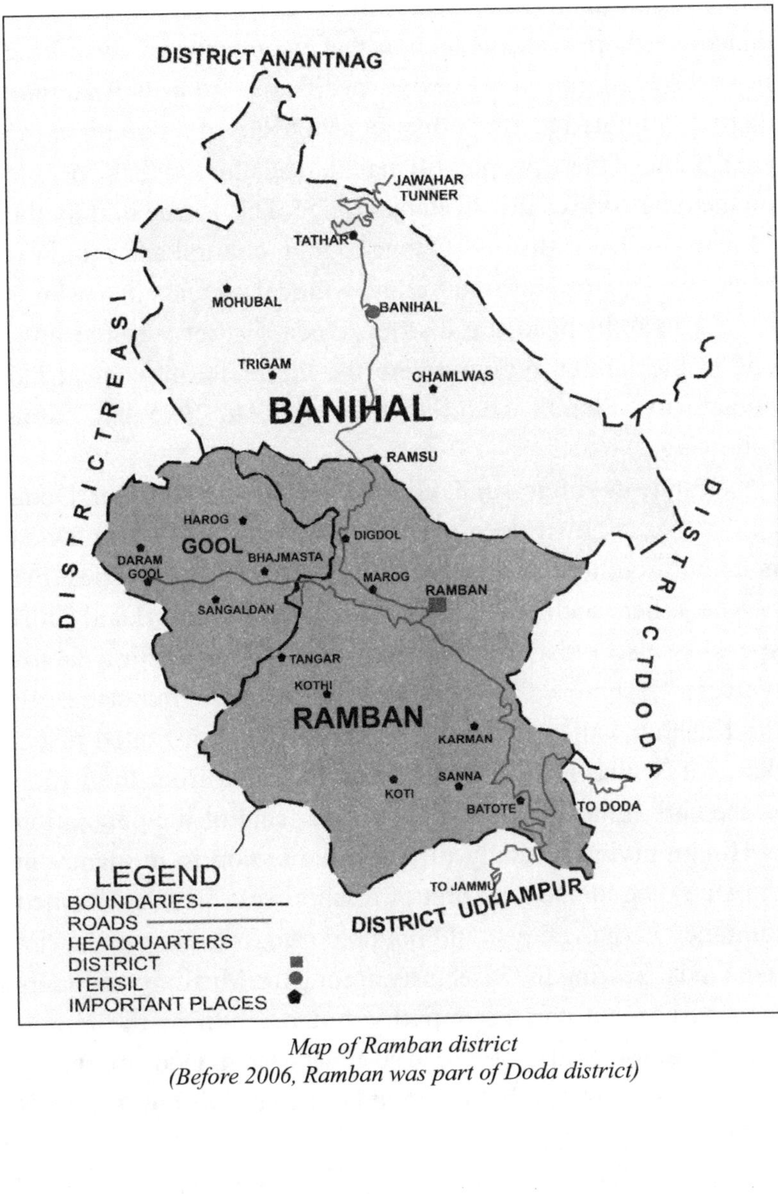

Map of Ramban district
(Before 2006, Ramban was part of Doda district)

rural parts, the dominant dialect is Siraji, which is different from Kashmiri. Approximately 40 per cent of the population is of Kashmiri origin in the district and speaks Kashmiri or one of its dialects. Historical accounts show that many centuries ago people from the Kashmir valley, more specifically from its Anantnag district, migrated to Doda district as a result of a famine in the area. Some of these people still maintain relations with the people on the other side of the Pir Panjal range. This is true of only the Muslims of Doda district. Owing to their cultural and religious affinities with the Kashmir valley, political currents in Kashmir have also influenced the district. Doda district was the only one in the Jammu region where the Plebiscite movement led defacto by Sheikh Abdullah from 1953 to 1975 had some following.

Despite its cultural and religious affinities to Kashmir, Doda culture has its own peculiarities. As discussed earlier, Doda is a multi-cultural society, where, besides Kashmiri speaking people, others such as Dogra, Bhaderwahi, Kishtwari and Padri speakers also exist. Further, the main distinguishing factor between Kashmir valley and Doda is the latter's minorities. In the Kashmir valley the minority population constituted just 5 per cent, which had almost entirely migrated from the valley in the early nineties. In Doda, 42.2 per cent of the population is Hindu, giving a totally different dimension to militancy in the area. The ideological diet of Kashmiriyat, which sustained militancy in the valley could not hold true for a diverse district like Doda. Seizing the insecurity among the Muslims, militants managed to get some sympathy, but reaction of the Hindu communal forces also provided sustenance to it. Doda militancy had a twin character that resorted both to its Kashmiri as well as Muslim character.

The Social Picture During the Attacks in Doda

The Gaddis (Hindu herders), initially, for mainly pecuniary motives, helped the local militants in the transportation of arms and ammunition. But the communal killings in the district created a feeling of distrust between the two communities (Hindus and Muslims), and the Gaddis emerged at that time as the main source of information for the security forces. As mentioned earlier, the initial communal killings were mainly the acts of local militants. Later, as foreign groups took over command of militant groups, the communal killings took an ideological colour. The objective behind the massacres of the Hindu community by the militants was to communalize the social fabric of Doda district.

Several other factors intervened to further communalize the environment.The militants justified each massacre as an act of revenge. The security forces did act in a haphazard manner at times. For instance, tensions ran high in Doda town after an Imam was allegedly tortured by the armed forces in Bhagwa area. The troops ran amuck after they suffered casualties on several occasions.[3]

Militant Groups in Doda

The first militant organization in Doda district was the Muslim Janbaaz. Its leader was Firdous Baba, popularly known as Babar Badr. He later bade goodbye to the armed struggle. Firdous Baba was the first person from Doda to have crossed the LoC. In Doda district, most of the militant groups had pro-Pakistan ideological leanings. Doda has links with Jammu city. Several young people from Doda district came to Jammu city for higher studies and they continue to maintain links with their native places. During this period some of them joined militant groups. However, Pro-Azadi groups like the JKLF were conspicuous by their absence in the district. Militancy was dominated by groups inclined towards Pakistan, and they engineered most of the massacres of Hindu civilians in Doda district. Intra-militant-group gun battles to gain supremacy were and are still common in Doda district. The two groups that have fought each other several times in the past are the Hizbul Mujahideen, dominated by a local cadre, and the Lashkar-e-Toiba, commanded mainly by foreigners.

Active Militancy Operations in Doda

It is difficult to trace the exact year when mass recruitment of militants from the district started. Given their close ethnic relations with the Kashmir valley, Doda residents were watching the events in the Kashmir valley closely. In the initial phase, Doda was used more as a sanctuary by the militants, as it provided a large terrain to hide in. But according to information and details given by the residents of the area, in 1990 itself the militants started their recruitment drive albeit at a very low level, mainly in the towns of Doda and Bhaderwah. The district shares its borders with Ladakh, the Kashmir valley, the rest of Jammu region and Himachal Pradesh. Firdous Baba, former commander of the banned militant outfit, Muslim Janbaaz, says, 'By 1993, on the basis of information shared by former militants, about 50 youth had already received training from across the LoC in Pakistan-administered Jammu and Kashmir.'

Even before the sensational massacres by the militants, indications of the coming violence were discernable. There was a blast in Bhaderwah in 1990 that blew up a bridge. The ammunition used was made from the local raw material used in building roads and was not imported from outside. At the same time, there was an attack on a video parlour in the main Doda town injuring one person. The primary motive of the attack was cultural policing by the militants. There was also a bank robbery in the district. A French engineer, Silva Antonia, was abducted on October 14, 1991 in Kishtwar at the Dul Hasti Hydroelectric project by the pro-Pakistan Al-Fateh militant outfit, leading to a temporary suspension of the project. In December 1992, the pro-Pakistan Harkat-ul-Mujahideen attacked a police post at Chhattroo in northern Doda district. On February 26, 1993 a central industrial security force camp at Shalimar in Kishtwar was the target of the militants. The first active local militant shot dead in Doda district was Nazir, a resident of Doda town, in 1993. His funeral was attended by many people and his body was buried in a local graveyard. This started the interference by militants in Doda's social fabric.

The Official View of Militancy in Doda

The official view treated militancy in Doda as an offshoot of militancy in the valley, which was expected to die out automatically if it was crushed in the Kashmir valley. The attack on bus passengers in Sarthal in Bhaderwah area of Doda district on August 1, 1993, when 17 Hindus on the bus were segregated and killed, was a watershed for militancy in the state and also for the security strategy, which had to move away from its Kashmir fixation. The first mass killing of Hindus by militants was based on a local initiative and not on the directions of the commanders across the LoC. Haji, the main conspirator behind the killing of the bus passengers, was a local person, educated in Jammu city. The attack was carried out owing mainly to a desire to sensationalize the movement, and according to disclosures by former militants, even they did not have any idea about the consequences of the inhuman act. Haji later went to Pakistan-administered Jammu and Kashmir for training and thereafter did not operate in Doda. He was finally killed in an operation in the Kashmir valley.

The event, as expected, had its repercussion on Doda's society. The incident shocked the nation as the entire character of militancy had changed. In political terminology, it was transformation from a militant movement in the state, based on Kashmiri nationalism, to Islamic ideology. The massacre did not go unnoticed in Doda's religiously diverse society. It provoked the migration of Hindus to the neighbouring area of Chamba in Himachal Pradesh. A communal fallout was the natural consequence of such militant activity that targeted the minority community. The communal profile of Doda district is very complex. The district has a Muslim majority, but within it there are Hindu-dominated tehsils. Therefore, any perceived injustice to a member of one community provokes a backlash on the other community. The communal killings, thus, created 'a sense of insecurity' among the minorities, both Muslim and Hindu, in their respective areas.

A Political Vacuum in Doda

When militancy started in Doda, the state was under President's rule, which had created a political vacuum in the district. Most of the officers in the upper echelons of the civilian administration belonged to other parts of the state and, therefore, had little understanding of the situation in Doda. In this insecure milieu, the Hindus increased their dependence on security forces and the Muslims, in turn, on the militants. During the same period, Hindu leaders demanded that Doda be declared a disturbed area and handed over to the army. In contrast the Muslims were apprehensive about such a move. A vicious circle of communalism and militancy started feeding on each other.

Another event, which vitiated the situation in Doda's political landscape, was the killing of Santosh Thakur, the district president of the BJP, in 1993. It was the first political killing in the district that further widened the communal gulf, changing the situation for the worse. That was when a national party like the BJP joined the demand to declare Doda a disturbed area, and hand it over to the army. This resulted in isolating the Muslims of the district from the rest of the country, as no political party in the country intervened to secularize the environment. An attempt however was initiated by Balraj Puri, who invited a Gandhian team led by Nirmala Deshpande to work for one month. The local people of the area say that this was the first time someone let them air their grievances.[4] But the peace was short-lived as one massacre after another hit the headlines.

On January 5, 1996, 16 Hindu villagers at Barshalla were killed. The year 1998 will go down as one of bloody massacres in the district. The blood trail started with the killing of 25 members of a wedding procession at Champnari near Doda town on June 19, 1998. The then Indian Home Minister and BJP leader, L.K. Advani, visited the spot and promised additional troops in the district. The Minister stated that the ruler who could not protect his subjects did not have the right to rule.

Subsequently, on July 28, militants murdered 16 Hindu villagers in the Kishtwar villages of Thakrain-Hor and Sarwan. On August 8, militants shot dead 34 road construction workers in the Kalaban area of Chamba district in Himachal Pradesh, adjoining the borders of Doda district. It demonstrated the dangerous dimension militancy had acquired in the region. On July 19, 1999, a year later, 15 Hindus were massacred in Layata area. The next year on August 2, 2000, they massacred 11 Hindus in Doda district. The year 2001 was remarkably similar to 1998. Eight Hindus were massacred in the Atholi area of Kishtwar tehsil on May 10, 2001; militants killed 20 Hindus in two separate massacres in Kishtwar area on July 22, 2001. On August 5, 2001 they killed 15 Hindus in the remote Sarote Dhar area of Doda.

After this series of massacres, on August 8, 2001, Jammu, Doda, Udhampur and Kathua were declared Disturbed Areas and brought under the Armed Forces (J&K) Special Powers Act, 1990. With this, the entire state, barring the Ladakh region, came under the Special Powers Act giving the armed forces a free hand to tackle militancy, since the two remaining districts of Jammu, Rajouri and Poonch, and the entire Kashmir valley were already covered by the Act.

The Role of the Village Defence Committee and Its Effects on Society

The Village Defence Committee (VDC) is a government devised mechanism to safeguard the local villagers. They are provided arms and rudimentary training to thwart militant attacks. A VDC comprises of four or more members who are recruited as Special Police Personnel on a monthly stipend. Usually VDC members are provided with .303 rifles. The main reason for the formation of VDCs in Doda district was because the security circles realized that it was virtually impossible to provide security to all parts of the large, hilly terrain of Jammu region, particularly the sprawling Doda district. Since protecting minorities was the immediate challenge before the authorities, mass recruitment of Hindus into VDCs was started in Doda.Arming the Hindus had its own implications. As mentioned earlier, Doda district is communally sensitive. Though Muslims have an edge over Hindus in demographic terms, the difference is marginal. In remote areas, arming the VDCs, accompanied by a lack of discipline in its ranks, created a sense of insecurity among the Muslims. The militants exploited this fear and portrayed themselves as the defenders of the Muslim community. They, in fact, justified many of the massacres in the district on the pretext of righting the alleged wrongdoings by the VDCs.

The first major attack on a VDC occurred when militants mowed down 15 members of three families at Layata, a ten kilometre walk from Thatri on the Doda-Kishtwar highway. The group was targeted for its support for and participation in the VDC activities. There would have been more people killed had it not been for the bravery shown by six residents including three children – Amrik Singh, Bhushan Kumar and Ramesh Kumar. The six residents took the guns into their hands and kept the militants engaged the whole night till the security forces arrived at the scene.

Notes

1. Prior to 2006, there were six districts of Jammu province or region.
2. Choudhary, Shabir, *Kashmir and the 1965 War* (Institute of Kashmir Affairs, London – United Kingdom), p. 3. 'Mujahideen' is the term used by the author for the infiltrators who were pushed in by the Pakistan army. Azad Kashmir is the official Pakistani name of Pakistan-administered Jammu and Kashmir in Pakistan. It is called 'Azad' by Pakistan to denote that it enjoys the status of an independent country.
3. In mid-2002, the forces burnt an entire village in the Marmat area after their commander was killed in an Improvised Explosive Device blast, forcing the people to migrate to Doda town, but the security forces denied the charge.
4. Interview with Abdul Qayoom Zargar, a social activist, based in Doda.

Lashkar militant eliminated in a combined operation of J&K Police and VDC personnel in Doda district in 2007 (Photograph by Luv Puri)

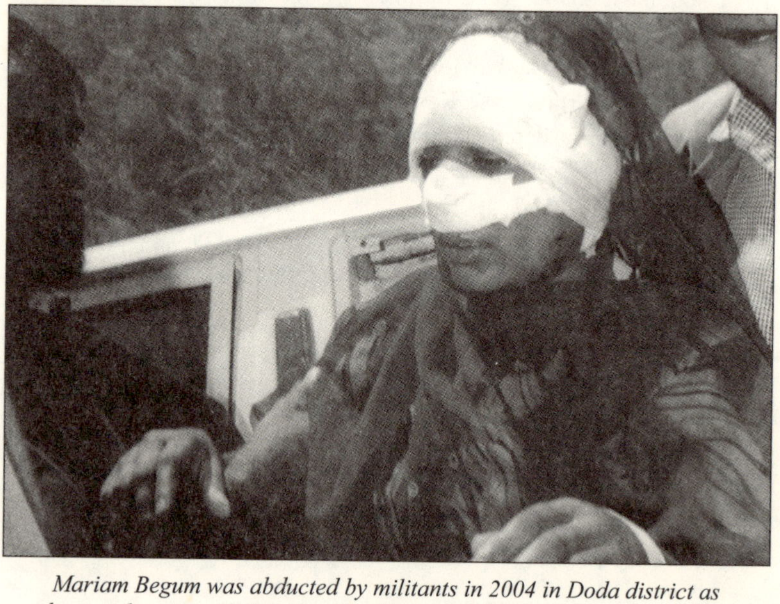

Mariam Begum was abducted by militants in 2004 in Doda district as she was the sister of Abdul Latif, a former militant who had surrendered. In retaliation militants abducted Mariam and tortured her for 25 days. Her ears and nose were chopped off before releasing her. (Photograph: Courtesy Ministry of Defence)

3

Initiation of Militancy in the Border Districts

Militancy reached Poonch district, adjoining Pakistan-administered Jammu and Kashmir, much after it arrived in Kashmir and Jammu's Doda district even though it was one of the main entry points from across the LoC to J&K, and its hilly terrain was far more suitable to the militants than the plains of the Valley.

Judging by the incidents reported and the views of the people of the district, militancy failed to take root even as late as 1996. Prior to 1996, the local people acted as guides for the armed militants coming into the Indian territory and showing them the routes to the Kashmir valley or Doda district. Infiltration continued on a daily basis, though violent incidents in the interiors were not uncommon. The historic importance of the district lies in the fact that it falls on the famous Mughal road, which was the traditional link between the Kashmir valley and the rest of the country.[1] More than half of the pre-1947 Poonch district is at present part of Pakistan-administered Jammu and Kashmir. Poonch had the status of a jagir within the state until 1946, when Maharaja Hari Singh made it a part of Jammu province.

The oft repeated issue of divided families living either side of LoC is most relevant to this part of the state, because the

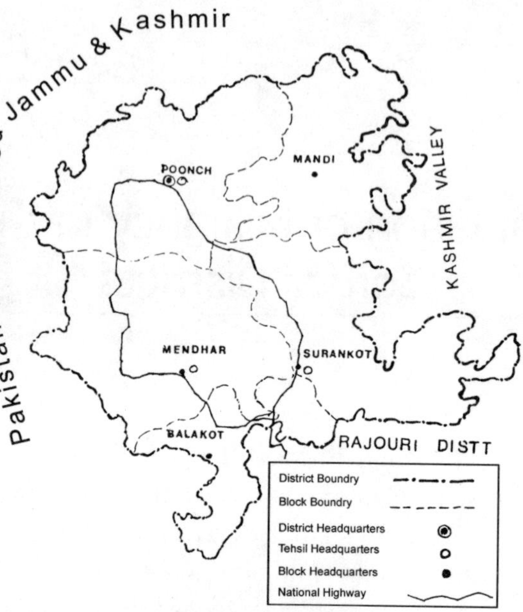

Map of Poonch district

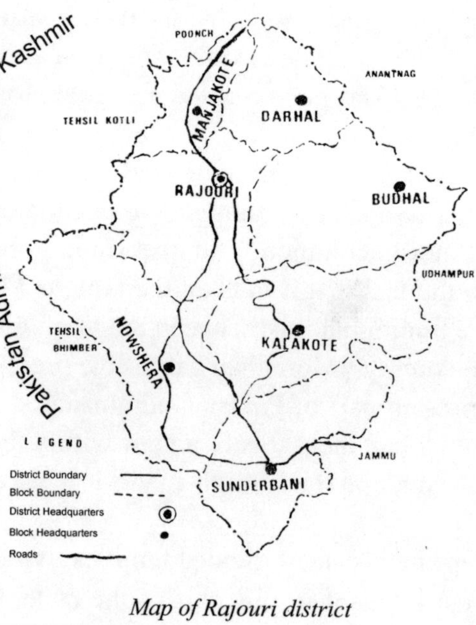

Map of Rajouri district

Indian troops patrolling along the LoC in Poonch district (Photography: Courtesy Ministry of Defence)

Indian troops patrolling along the LoC in Poonch district (Photograph: Courtesy Ministry of Defence)

Kashmir valley was not divided in 1947. In Poonch, villages and families were divided. Therefore, War between the two countries always has the greatest impact on this district. The Kashmiri revolt failed to inspire the people of Poonch district, which has its own distinct culture. The ethnic barrier between Poonch and Kashmir is more formidable than the 3353 metres high geographical barrier of the Pir Panjal range. Local recruitment by militant groups in this district started when the non-Kashmiri-speaking militants from Pakistan-administered J&K and Pakistan arrived on the Indian side of J&K. They were termed as 'foreign' but that is a misnomer since most of the militants in this category belong to Pakistan-administered Jammu and Kashmir, who are part of the same ethnic stock as the people of Poonch. A 'foreign militant', who is an alien in the valley owing to his different ethnicity, may well be at home while he is in this border district.

Migration Across the Line of Control

As people of the same ethnic stock live on both sides of the Line of Control, a certain amount of trans-LoC migration is a common feature. However the migration became more frequent during times of disturbance. In normal times, migration occurs because of economic reasons. Mendhar is one of the sectors in Poonch district where migration across the LoC has been most rampant. During the months of April to July 1991 there was a sudden spurt in migration, particularly in Panjani area where over 400 men, women and children went across to Pakistan-administered Jammu and Kashmir. Such incidents of exfiltration usually increase in border tensions.

During the tensions at the border after the Parliament attack on December 13, 2001, migration across the LoC again witnessed an increase. Muslim Rajputs were the predominant migrants.

This community is one of the main power-wielders in Pakistan-administered Jammu and Kashmir. This illegal crossing of the population assumes importance, because these migrants act as guides for militants and provide them with vital information about which routes to follow. The illegal crossing of civilians subsided, after fencing of the Line of Control started in 2002.

The Specifics of Militancy in Poonch District

The two assembly constituencies of the Poonch district, that is Mendhar and Poonch Haveli, fall right on the borders. Surankote forms an arc behind these two constituencies, and before Operation Sarp Vinash started in April, 2003, it was a hotbed of militancy. This is an area, which even in defence circles was known as the 'liberated' zone.

Surankote: A 'Liberated' Zone

Militancy in Poonch district revolved around the Surankote assembly constituency. In terms of area, it is the largest assembly constituency and has scattered population. It touches the Kashmir valley on one side and is called the 'highway of militancy', stretching from the northwest of Jammu region to the northeast district of Doda along the southern side of the Pir Panjal. The geographical divide of the river Suran marks the difference in intensity of militancy. The hilly belt beyond the river Suran was regarded as a security planner's nightmare. After Operation Sarp Vinash, militancy was almost wiped out in this belt. Operation Sarp Vinash was started in April 2003, when local Gujjar Muslims backed by the army and the police troops revolted against the militants. The operation succeeded in clearing the area of militants, though its exact success in terms of militants killed contested by different sources.[2]

Poonch's Ethnic Profile

In order to understand the local characteristics of militancy in Poonch, we must have some idea of the demographic profile in which the militants operate. The district falls on the Mughal road. Diverse people belonging to different areas have made it their home over a period of time. It is a Muslim-dominated district, but here the religious homogeneity is broken by ethnic diversity. It would not be wrong to say that it is the ethnic diversity of the district which has shaped its post-independence history and which also left its impact on the character of militancy in the area. The communities that dominate the area include Rajputs Muslims, Gujjars and Bakerwals, Syeds, Mughals and pockets of Kashmiri-speaking people.[3]

After the central government awarded the Gujjars and Bakerwals the status of Scheduled Tribes in 1991, the non-Gujjars of Rajouri and Poonch came together to demand the same. Their nomadic lifestyle gives the Gujjars and Bakerwals a distinct identity. What bonds the non-Gujjars of different religions and castes is the Pahari language spoken in the area. The name 'Pahari' in the context of this state has been misunderstood in many respects. Usually Paharis are wrongly believed to be people who live in the mountains. On the contrary, in Poonch, it is a linguistic identity. Barring Gujjars and Bakerwals who speak Gojri, the others speak Pahari. The small Kashmiri-speaking populace also lives in villages like Poshana, Mandi and Loran villages. However, they have been indigenized and are equally conversant with Pahari.

The two dominant groups of the Paharis and Gujjars have asserted themselves in the political battleground. In the elections in the recent past the polarization was demonstrated in a glaring manner, when the Gujjar community voted for the

Gujjar candidate and the Paharis voted for the Pahari candidate, irrespective of party affiliations. Relations between the two communities have further worsened with the Pahari community clamouring for the status of a Scheduled Tribe, similar to the Gujjars. The Gujjars were given this status in 1991 by the Centre during the short-lived Chandrashekhar government, through an ordinance that was later ratified by Parliament.

Delayed Response to Militancy in Poonch

Fierce encounters along the LoC in the Poonch sector were a common feature in the early 1990s with the increasing infiltration of Kashmiri-speaking militants. The Indian forces were able to track down these militants even in the interior, while they were on their way back to the valley. For instance, in a major operation on July 17, 1990, about 33 militants who had crossed Sauji area in Mandi, Poonch district, were gunned down. All of them were

Members of the Gujjar tribe (Photograph by Luv Puri)

Kashmiri-speaking and belonged to the Pulwama and Anantnag districts of the valley.

Militancy started taking root in Poonch from 1996 when militants started attacking security personnel. At that time, security planners described this trend as an attempt by the militants to ensure that the road to the Kashmir valley and Doda stayed open for them. Eventually Poonch district became an active zone where militants started carrying out their regular operations as they did in the valley. Their clear purpose was to recruit local people to their ranks, which they could not do until 1996. The delayed response to militancy in Poonch was, as discussed earlier, on account of the ethnic gap between Kashmir and Poonch. In an interview with me, former J&K Chief Secretary, S.S. Bloeria, a Dogra, recalls an incident that confirms this assertion. Once a Gujjar came to his office for help, he in turn directed the Gujjar to the bureaucrat in charge of the area, who was a co-religionist. The Gujjar categorically stated that as the area officer was a Kashmiri he would not understand his problem but 'as you are closer to us, you will do justice to us'.

Even in the past, the two parts of the state, though sharing religious affinity, have responded differently to historic events. The first revolt in the state against the Dogra monarchy took place in 1947 in the erstwhile Poonch jagir in Bagh tehsil. This coincided with a tribal attack on Kashmir, sponsored by Abdul Qayoom Khan, the Chief Minister of the North West Frontier Province, which the people of the Kashmir valley resisted.

Similarly, in the 1965 war, infiltrators got sufficient support from the local population of Poonch district and they were able to win a large tract of land. Even local commanders were appointed, and they declared themselves independent of Indian rule.[4] This was in sharp contrast to Kashmir, where the infiltrators received no such response both in the 1947 and 1965 Indo-Pakistan wars.

In the present era, militancy became common to both parts of the state only in the mid-nineties.

Alienation in Poonch

The reasons for the positive response to militancy in the district are multi-fold. Poonch was well connected to prosperous cities of undivided Punjab like Rawalpindi before the Partition. But after 1947, it was isolated due to the creation of new boundaries. Movement on one side was blocked by the security forces along the LoC. The district suffered administratively and economically, as it was at a great distance from the capital cities of Jammu and Srinagar. Employment opportunities in the district thereby were a bare minimum.

Internal connectivity within the district was also not developed after the Partition. Unlike the plains and the accessible Kashmir valley, the remote hamlets of Poonch to date have not been brought into the road network. In matters of necessities and other infrastructure, like electricity, the district was given low priority.

Political Factors

Political factors causing the start of militancy in the district are also worth examining. Cultural pride was always a cementing factor between the Hindus and Muslims of Poonch district and its separate identity as a jagir. Immediately after its merger with the state, popular discontent and aspirations were represented by Ghulam Qadir Bandey, popularly known as Sher-e-Poonch. He symbolized a secular Poonchi identity. But after his death the district was pushed into a political vacuum that no political party in the state had the vision or ability to fill. Thus, a space was created for communal politics, which was exploited by the militants who came across the LoC with their fanatic religious and jehadi mindsets.

This was in contrast to the earlier phase of militancy that was distinctively Kashmiri in character. Further, the fact that the militants coming across the LoC belonged broadly to Pothwari speaking communities[5] that extend up to Islamabad, the capital of Pakistan, struck a chord with the same ethnic stock on this side of the LoC. These militants, the 'foreigners', received shelter from a section of the local Muslim population of Poonch in the early stages, and later received their active support. Once a section of the local population got emotionally involved with the changing phase of militancy, which merged religion with ethnic appeal, it did not take long for Poonch to become a hot-bed of militancy.

Besides these factors there was the added factor of the martial character of the people living in Poonch. During Dogra rule, Poonch provided one of the highest recruitments to the army. More importantly, its contribution to the British army was the largest in terms of proportion of population in British India. It did not take the martial communities of Poonch long to join the armed militant movement. Muslim Rajputs were attracted to the other side of the LoC where Rajputs had cornered political power and major benefits. This exercised a strong psychological pull on the Muslim Rajputs on this side of the LoC.

Despite professing the same religion, the two communities of the Rajputs and Gujjars are very different from each other. Traditionally, Muslim Rajputs controlled power centres in the area. Their relations with the Gujjars were far from cordial, the Rajputs being ruling elite looked down on the pastoral people, that is, the nomads.The antagonism between the Rajputs and the Gujjars widened further when the latter were given the status of a Scheduled Tribe by the Government of India in 1991. Similarly, the Gujjars too, in the year 1997 became dissatisfied when they were denied political representation in the state cabinet during Farooq Abdullah's National Conference rule. None of the three Muslim majority constituencies in Poonch had a Gujjar MLA. All three Muslim ministers from Poonch, as well as those from the adjoining districts of Rajouri, in the state cabinet were from the Pahari speaking community. The community was represented in the state ministry for many years by a Minister of State elected from the Kashmir region, whereas earlier, its representation used to be larger with at least one cabinet minister from the district. The loyalty of the discontented Gujjar community thus could no longer be taken for granted.

Intra-Militant Rivalries

The recruitment to the militants' ranks from the Gujjar Muslims of the district could have been due to religious affinity, but the ethnic differences undoubtedly left its imprint on the consequences. To take one illustration, the first militancy-related incident in the district was the killing of 20 family members in the Sailan area near Surankote. This incident was a direct consequence of an intra-group fight in which a Gujjar militant, Zakir Hussain was killed by a Pahari militant Imitiaz on August 3rd, 1998. Hussain was killed because he was suspected to have become an informer for the security forces. He was an active militant and had received training from across the border. Imtiaz's family fearing a reprisal, took refuge in the house of Muhammad Shabir Sheikh. According to an eyewitness account, on the night of August 3, a group of Gujjars swooped down on Muhammad Shabir Sheikh's house. Every member of the family was asked to line up. Imtiaz's parents were shot first. To ensure that there was no eyewitness of the incident everyone present was killed, including six children and a pregnant woman. The brutality can be imagined from the fact that after killing Imtaiz's parents, their bodies were chopped up.[6] The lone survivor of the massacre is Muhammad Shabir Sheikh, who was a teenager at that time. He survived because he had gone out to relieve himself. He witnessed the entire incident as he hid behind the bushes, while his entire family was being wiped out. Shabir identified the men and even met the then Indian Defence Minister, George Fernandes, and the Jammu and Kashmir Chief Minister, Farooq Abdullah, when they came to visit the site. Muhammad Shabir claims that he has been attacked several times by the culprits, as they fear that his survival will always remain a threat to them. Just two years after the massacre of his family, when he returned to his house, the militants approached him to join their ranks and take revenge on the Gujjars who were responsible for the tragedy. In another case of local rivalry at Morha Bachhi (again in Surankote constituency) in the month of August 1999, about 15 Muslims belonging to three Pahari families were killed. Those killed included five women and seven children. Two families were completely wiped out. The dispute was a result of rivalry between the Gujjars and the Paharis.

These examples clearly illustrate the role that gun plays in an environment of ethnic polarity where it becomes a tool to settle differences between ethnic groups. In fact, in many cases members of one ethnic group joined militant ranks so that they could assert their power through guns on the competing group. For instance, when Chowdhary Ghani, a Gujjar Congress block leader was killed by a group of Pahari militants, the Gujjars joined the rival militant ranks in large numbers, with the aim of taking revenge.

Contradictions Between Militants and the Local Culture

Many contradictions between the militants and the local culture came to the fore. Militants tried to capture the ground with the sole appeal of religion, with no respect or understanding of the local culture. This provoked a harsh reaction against them. For example, in Hari Marote on July 29, 1998, a foreign militant polished his shoes with a cloth tied to a Ziarat (burial place of a saint) that is revered by the local people. This provoked an instant reaction in the form of protest demonstrations against militants. A similar incident occurred at the Ziarat of Jammu Shaheed. Here foreign militants protested against the serving of food at an Urs ceremony (death anniversary of the saint) terming it un-Islamic. The local people resented this and there was a largely unreported backlash from them against the militants.

However, the militants tried to suppress these contradictions by resorting to sensational communal killings, claiming to be defenders of Islam. On July 1, 1999, nine Hindu villagers in Mendhar in Poonch district were killed. The cause had a local dimension. The marriage of a Muslim woman, Faheen Kauser, with a Hindu man, Shankar Lal, being the immediate reason, according to the local people. The Muslim community alleged that the girl had been kidnapped. In the absence of political and social institutions common to both communities that could have amicably resolved the misunderstanding, the militants took advantage of the situation and intervened by mowing down nine Hindu villagers.

They tried to suppress the contradictions between their ideology and local culture by increasingly resorting to communalizing the situation. In one of their sensational communal strikes, militants beheaded two Hindu priests after kidnapping them from a temple near Dhundhak bridge on the Surankote-Poonch road on August 28, 2001. As tension gripped the area, the authorities imposed an indefinite curfew in Poonch and Surankote to guard against the possible outbreak of communal violence. The state, in turn could not take advantage owing to the political and administrative vacuum. The local people were also angered by the atrocities committed by the security forces and the extremist outfits were quick to take advantage of this.

Rajouri

Present-day Rajouri district comprises some areas of erstwhile Mirpur district currently in Pakistan-administered Jammu and Kashmir and some areas of the present Reasi district. It was severely affected by the events of 1947. A part of the district in the south was bifurcated between India and Pakistan. The result was large scale migration from one part of the state to the other. While Hindus and Sikhs migrated from neighbouring districts like Mirpur, Poonch, Bhimber, Kotli (now in Pakistan-administered Jammu and Kashmir) and settled in different parts of Rajouri, many Muslim families migrated to the other side. After Partition, Rajouri became part of Poonch district, from which a new district called Rajouri was carved out in the late 1960s.

Rajouri district is hilly and comprises four assembly constituencies Nowshera, Kalakote, Rajouri and Dharhal – each with its own distinguished characteristics in terms of geographic, community and ethnic features. The district has four small towns of Rajouri, Nowshera, Sunderbani and Thanna Mandi. About 94.85 per cent of the population lives in villages. Most of the areas of present-day Rajouri district were taken over by Pakistani regulars or raiders in 1947 and were recaptured by the Indian army after the Maharaja signed the Instrument of Accession with India.

Rajouri's Strategic Location

The famous Mughal road passes through Rajouri before entering Poonch, and is, therefore of immense strategic value. The Mughal

Emperor, Jehangir, died in this district on his return journey from Kashmir. Even today, it is the main supplyline for the forward Poonch district. In the first Indo-Pak war in 1947-48, the district was the scene of action of one of the fiercest battles between the armies of the two countries. Rajouri was under the control of raiders for around six months before the Indian forces pushed them back successfully. The famous battle of Jhangar, where Brigadier Usman lost his life, was fought in Nowshera tehsil. Nowshera was earlier a part of Mirpur district presently in Pakistan-administered Jammu and Kashmir. The route to Mirpur was through Nowshera. A signboard can still be seen in this sector, showing the route to Mirpur.

The infiltration at Nowshera is comparatively less than the other sectors of the district. The reason is that the area is mainly inhabited by Hindus, and hence the infiltrators feel insecure passing through Nowshera. For the militants, Rajouri district as a whole is of considerable importance. As discussed earlier, it shares its borders with three other districts, namely Poonch, Reasi and Jammu. The Dharhal-Budhal-Mahore stretch is the 'highway' for the militants' journey to Doda district and the Reasi hills. When militancy started in the area, the Hindu community living on the higher grounds were targeted as they were suspected to be informers for the security forces. After the massacre of several Hindus, they migrated in large numbers and took refuge in Rajouri town or other parts of Jammu, where they could feel secure.

The Village Defence mechanism, first started in Doda, was replicated in Rajouri district. Most of the VDCs were concentrated in Budhal tehsil. The tehsil is hilly and provides safe routes for militants to venture deep into other districts for their operations. Most of the area in this tehsil is far from the nearest motorable road, and in many cases it took the forces atleast one day to reach the spot where massacres were committed. Keeping these facts in view, providing weapons to the vulnerable community alone could give security to the people. However, a few months after the constitution of the VDCs, the families of their personnel were specifically targeted. The .303 rifles given to VDC personnel were of no match with the militants' sophisticated weapons and the former suffered a high number of casualties.

Differences Between Rajouri and Poonch Districts

Rajouri district shares several similarities with Poonch, but it is considerably more diverse in terms of its religious and ethnic profile. Bimber Gali pass is a natural geographical barrier between Rajouri and Poonch districts. Unlike Poonch, which is largely Muslim majority, Rajouri district has a sizeable Hindu population with Muslims constituting just 58.28 per cent of the total population. Community-wise, Rajouri could be conveniently divided into two halves – North-west and South-east. In the South-east, Sunderbani, Kalakot and Nowshera tehsils are overwhelmingly populated by Hindus whereas the North-western tehsils of Rajouri, Thanna Mandi and Kotranka are predominantly Muslim, with a fair representation of Hindus in some villages. In Rajouri town, Hindus are in a majority in nine out of ten wards. Muslims almost exclusively inhabit the tenth ward.

Thus the distribution of Muslims and Hindus in Rajouri is very complex. In one particular area one community may be in a majority, but there may be several localities within that area where members of the other community are in a majority. Within the two communities there are caste divisions that sometimes override even religious differences. Of the four assembly constituencies, two – Kalakote and Dharhal – are located in the

Village Defence Committee in Rajouri district
(Photograph by Luv Puri)

Locally recruited Special Police Officers undergoing training
(Photograph by Luv Puri)

interior of the district. Kalakote is mainly Hindu majority but with a high concentration of the nomadic Gujjar community.

Similarly, the constituency of Nowshera, which falls along the LoC, has a Hindu majority with a large concentration of Gujjars, but the population ratio in each tehsil is different. In the interiors, Dharhal is a Muslim-dominated segment but here the caste divide between the Gujjars and Paharis is sharp. This is substantiated by the fact that in the 2002 assembly elections, a little known Hindu Pahari candidate, Thakur Puran Singh, trounced a Muslim Gujjar candidate belonging to a politically important family. Caste and religious lines, therefore cut across each other.

Militancy in Rajouri District

The heterogeneity in Rajouri gives militancy a slightly different character from that in Poonch district. The main centres of militancy in the district are in the interior tehsils like Dharhal, Budhal, Thanna Mandi and in the outer areas of Rajouri town. Sometimes the militants make their presence felt in areas with a Hindu majority, like Kalakote and Nowshera. In the first two years of militancy in Rajouri, the militants used the hilly terrain of the district, especially in the Budhal tehsil to reach the hills of Reasi, that is, Mahore and Gool, and further up to Doda district, using the passes to enter the Kashmir valley. The interiors of Rajouri district, particularly the Thanna Mandi-Budhal tract, are mainly hilly and heavily forested. This facilitates safe passage for the militants. It was in this tract that they first encountered the security forces when the latter, in a well-planned operation, tried to block the militants' routes in the late 1990s.

In the initial period, there were direct encounters between the militants and the security forces. For instance, in the month of September 1997, the militants engaged the army positions around Thanna Mandi directly by occupying the heights of

Ratan Pir, and fired mortars. It took the army an entire week to clear the area, and in the resulting encounters over a score of militants were killed, while the army lost a major, a JCO and a jawan. The attack was intense and eyewitnesses recall that 50 militants were active in four villages. But soon the militants started attacking the newly constituted VDCs in the isolated hilly areas of the district.

These were targeted killings. Militants struck Swari village in Budhal tehsil in a big way on September 24, 1997, killing eight Hindus and wounding four others. This was one of the first major strikes against Hindus in the hilly belt.

In later years, the pattern changed further, with militants attacking Hindus in the remote hills, on the suspicion that they were involved with VDCs. On February 19, 1998, the day Prime Minister Vajapyee started his Lahore Bus Yatra, they killed 20 Hindu villagers in Bal Jaralan, Khorbani and Bharyana villages in Rajouri and the neighbouring Reasi district. Six Hindus were killed in Kot Dhara in Rajouri on August 19, 2000. These incidents increased the insecurity among the Hindus in the scattered hills. The militants became even more brutal, making women and children their direct victims. Sometimes they targeted the families of those involved in VDCs. For instance, five minors and two women were among eight people killed in the Dharamsal area of Kalakote assembly constituency on February 18, 2002. They also made their way into areas of the district that had large Hindu majorities. Four Hindus were massacred in Nowshera in Kanara Chowkian village on August 31, 2001.

Migration from Rajouri

Hindus started migrating from the remote villages after the Swari massacre in the month of September 1997 in which eight people were killed. Villagers migrated to safer places from Mangota,

Upper Mangota, Kalal, Uppar Kalal, Baljarala, Dalouri in Rajouri and also certain villages in Thanna Mandi tehsil. Families took refuge in Rajouri town or Jammu city. These people still have not returned to their villages. Besides, several families stayed either in the homes of their relatives or in rented accommodations in the town. Though migration in certain pockets was a major fallout of militancy, several continued to live in isolated areas, despite heavy odds.

Attacks on the Muslim Community in Rajouri

Eventually, even the Muslim community was not spared. In a gruesome incident on February 10, 2001, fifteen people of three families of VDC members, including three women and seven children, were burnt alive when militants, after locking them inside their houses, set them ablaze at village Morasalahi of Kot Charwal, 40 kilometres from the Budhal area of Rajouri district. All the people killed were Gujjar Muslims and they were killed on the mere suspicion of being informers for the security forces and for forming a VDC.

There were also attacks on political leaders and their relatives. On August 18, 1998, two relatives of the former Speaker of the J&K Assembly Mirza Abdul Rashid were killed in Dandhoke near Darhal. The militants also targeted the J&K police force. In one devastating attack, 17 people consisting of 13 police personnel, two medical assistants and two civilians were killed in the Kyoli jungles of Manjakote on March 2, 2001. Harsh punishments for informers was not only limited to men but extended to women as well. On the night of September 2, 1999 they slaughtered a young girl in the Gujjar Mandi area of Rajouri district on the charge that she had links with the security forces. Militants (belonging to the Al-Badr outfit) killed three Muslim girls on December 19, 2002, in Hasyote village on the suspicion of having provided information to the forces.

After the people, including Muslims, expressed their resentment against these killings, one group of militants, the Jaish-e-Mohammad, apologized.

The Effect of Militancy on Society in Rajouri

Rajouri district, with a religiously heterogeneous society and affected by militancy, could not remain untouched by the communal virus. In the last decade, communal tensions have occasionally erupted into violence. Tensions are more pronounced in Rajouri town. This can be substantiated by the fact that a clear divide exists in the localities of Rajouri town, since both communities have been ghettoized in their separate zones. Several incidents of communal violence have been reported in the town during this period, sometimes over the most trivial issues.

The communal virus has even affected students and educational institutions. For instance, on September 17, 2000, curfew had to be imposed in the town following a clash between Hindu and Muslim students in the Government Degree College over a minor matter. A Hindu boy kicked a volleyball that Muslim boys were playing with in the college playgrounds. A quarrel erupted between the two groups of students with the event subsequently acquiring political overtones.

One of the reasons why communal tension has been mainly restricted to Rajouri town is because majority of the population came here after the Partition, or later from the forward areas during the 1965 and 1971 wars. Unlike Poonch district, where both Muslims and Hindus are proud of their common cultural identity, such a synthesis between the communities does not exist in Rajouri. The members of the two communities live in separate localities. Rajouri town has a Hindu majority and is surrounded by an overwhelming Muslim one. The response to every militancy-related incident gets a polarized reaction on the basis of religion. For instance, there will be an instant shutdown of Rajouri Bazaar after Hindus are killed even in a remote village. In the same vein, after every alleged killing of innocent Muslim by the forces there is a protest by the Muslims of the area.

Cultural Policing in the Border Districts

Militancy had an effect on some social customs and traditions. For instance, in the month of December 2002, the veil campaign was started in the district. Veiling was a completely unfamiliar practice for women in the district till then. The campaign had a local dimension to it as it followed an incident in Thanna Mandi where some orthodox Muslims took objection to boys and girls dancing together at a college picnic. Thereafter, militants stepped in to take advantage and asked the people to comply. Their writ had an impact, and for the first time in the known history of the district, the veil became the norm for women, though the campaign fizzled out after some time. However, during the short period when the campaign was at its peak, the Hindus in the district were frightened, as they perceived it to be the start of Muslim fundamentalism. As more and more women of the district complied and wore the veil, the Hindus were increasingly alarmed. It was basically the result of the reaction and fear of the Hindus, that the media characterized it as Talibanization. This nomenclature, in turn, reinforced the fear of the local Hindus. However, due to the opposition of the Muslim community, cultural policing failed to have an impact.

Notes

1. The importance of the old Mughal Road is based on the fact that it was the only entry point to the Kashmir valley from the rest of India.

The road originated in Jhelum town in Punjab (now in Pakistan) and then touched Kotli (in Pakistan-administered Jammu and Kashmir), Thanna Mandi (Rajouri district) and finally Chandimarh, located on the Pir Panjal range, while one branch crossed over to Shopian via Heer Pora in the Kashmir valley.

2. The army claimed to have killed more than 60 militants in the Hill Kaka area of Marrah village in Surankote, whereas the First Information Report of the J&K Police at Surankote police station in Poonch district did not reflect this figure. The army was accused of inflating the number of militants killed.
3. Gujjars and Bakerwals belong to the same ethnic group and speak the same language, hence little distinction is made between the two. In J&K, the difference between the Gujjars and the Bakerwals is not ethnic but occupational. The names of the communities are based on their occupations – Bakerwals rear goats or 'bakri' in the local parlance, and Gujjars rear buffaloes.
4. Interviews with the local people.
5. Pahari is one of the languages that belongs to the broader Pothwari group of languages. The Pothwari belt includes Pakistan-administered Jammu and Kashmir and districts of Jammu region and the Kashmir valley which adjoin Pakistan-administered Jammu and Kashmir.
6. Interview with the survivor.
7. Indian and Pakistani troops have observed a ceasefire along the LoC since November 26, 2003 till today.

4

Highway Routes

After discussing the ups and downs of militancy in Doda, Rajouri and Poonch, this chapter discusses its impact on the hilly areas of Udhampur, Reasi and Kathua. These areas are on the highway to Doda and Kishtwar, and constitute the third zone to fall under militancy. Within the tehsils of these districts that have a Hindu majority, there are villages that have a high concentration of Muslims, and vice versa. For instance, Ramnagar tehsil in Udhampur district has a Hindu majority, but the Dudu and Basantgarh blocs have a high concentration of Muslims. Similarly, Mahore tehsil of Reasi district has villages that have a Hindu majority. Rajput Hindus live in significant numbers in the hills of Mahore in Reasi district and Dudu-Basantgarh in Udhampur district, where militancy is rife. Gaddis (Hindu shepherds) also inhabit these hilly tracts in the eastern parts of Udhampur district. Most of the Muslims belong to the Gujjar community and are spread across the district, with Kashmiri-speaking Muslims in some pockets. The latter are concentrated in Mahore tehsil of Reasi district bordering the Kashmir region.

At the social level, the rivalry between the Gujjars and the Kashmiri-speaking Muslims is intense due to differences in social customs and traditions. The Gujjar community, as is the case in the rest of the state, has its own distinctive nomadic culture and

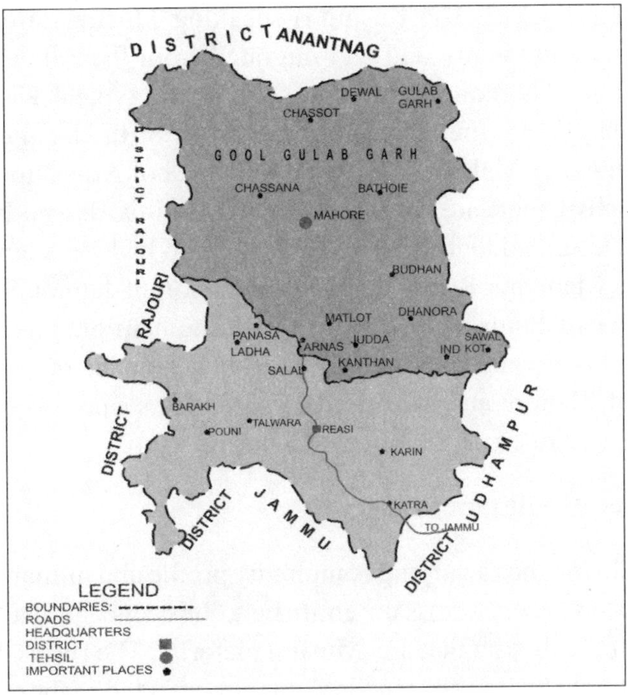

Reasi district (Before 2006, Reasi was part of Udhampur district)

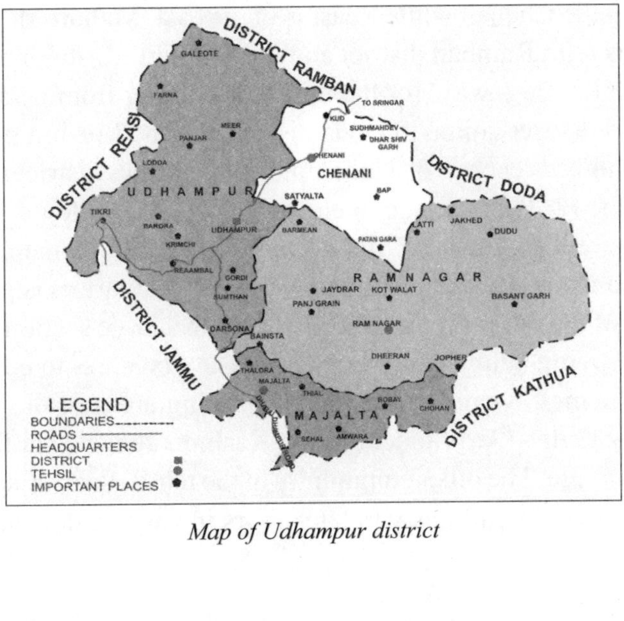

Map of Udhampur district

language (Gojri). The Kashmiri-speaking Muslims are not a nomadic community and had migrated from the valley many years ago. The community still follows the typical Kashmiri lifestyle, though they have absorbed some of the local culture also. In lower Mahore, particularly the area of Arnas, touching Reasi tehsil, there are pockets of Dogra Muslims, descendants of Mian Deedo, a Dogra guerrilla general who had led a rebellion against Maharaja Ranjit Singh's occupation of Jammu.[1] When the ruler of Punjab killed Deedo with the help of Raja Gulab Singh, his descendants fled to take shelter under the Muslim ruler of Mahore and converted to Islam to escape persecution by the new rulers of Jammu and Kashmir.[2]

Spheres of Militancy in Reasi

Reasi district has a varying community profile and militancy has not spread evenly across the entire belt.[3] It is concentrated in the parts of the district that are Muslim majority. The river Chenab is a natural border between the militancy-affected Mahore tehsil and the relatively peaceful Reasi tehsil. Mahore is located to the west of the Chenab while Reasi is on its east. Mahore shares its borders with Ramban district and the southern Kashmir region. It is on the 'highway' for the militants coming from Budhal of Rajouri district going to Doda district and the Muslim pockets in the upper reaches of Udhampur and Kathua districts; or to cross the Pir Panjal range to enter the Kashmir valley.

The entire tehsil of Mahore is a mountainous patch. The road connectivity even within the tehsil headquarters is poor. It is one of the poorest parts of the state with a large section of the people living below the poverty line. The first areas to be hit by the militancy were the Kashmiri-speaking areas of the tehsil, namely Gulab Garh, touching the Kashmir region, via the Pir Panjal range. The other community in the tehsil, the Gujjars also got involved in militancy in later years in varying degrees.

The Importance of Mahore Tehsil in Reasi

Mahore was important for the militants as it is situated at a strategic location. From the early 1990s, the Kashmiri militants used this tract for their foot journey to the Kashmir valley from Rajouri district, bordering the LoC. However, the local Muslims of the tehsil got involved much later, mainly after the pro-Pakistan Hizbul Mujahideen took over from the pro-Azadi JKLF. Kashmiri speaking militants were the Hizbul Mujahideen's first recruits and several years later, in the late 1990s, a section of the Gujjars were also involved with them. In Mahore, the Hizbul Mujahideen dominates over all other militant organizations.

Security officials point out that it was the involvement of the Gujjars in the later years that gave militancy an impetus in the belt. Even the tacit support of the Gujjars of that belt was of immense importance for militancy as a whole. The Gujjars were more familiar with this hilly belt than any other community. They were useful to the militants in providing shelter and acting as guides, pointing out the trekking routes and safe passes.

In the initial period, the militants used the tract in Mahore tehsil as a 'highway' for their entry into Kashmir and the Doda district. They attacked the security forces to ensure that the road ahead remained safe for them. Later, they came down and targeted the vehicles of the security forces plying along the interior road network in Mahore tehsil. The tehsil has been an active zone for the militants where they have attacked police posts, BSF camps and detonated Improvised Explosive Devices on the roads. In later years, civilians were also targeted in the higher reaches. The aim was to clear any section of the population who they believed could be informers for the security forces. The first attacks were on the Hindus settled in the isolated hamlets in the hills. For instance, on August 15, 2001, while India was celebrating its Independence Day, the militants gunned down five old members of a Hindu family in remote Sahar Badoli village in Mahore. They struck the family when six of its members, including three women and two brothers, had gone to their dhoks (temporary shelters) in the upper reaches of Sahar Badoi to celebrate the Hindu festival of Janmashtmi (birthday of Lord Krishna) in an old temple.

The attacks on VDC members and their families were even more brutal. Four children of a member of a VDC, Gyan Singh in Shajru hamlet, were killed on December 1, 2000. His children, 15-year-old Hoshiar Singh, daughters Pinki Devi (12 years), Darshana (10 years) and Anju (three years) were killed. In the later stages, militants also attacked their co-religionists for their involvement with the security forces.

Personal Rivalries in Reasi

Militants also bring with them a sense of power. The local militants exploited this new-found power. In one incident, they massacred five members of a family belonging to Fateh Mohammad Gujjar at Budhan in the Gool area of Reasi district on March 23, 2000. The deceased belonged to a family of masons. Gujjar's family was targeted because he had demanded wages for the masonry work done by him in the house of the local militant, Mohammad Shaffi. After the work was completed, Shafi's family refused to pay his wages. Fateh Mohammad then approached the family's relatives and urged them to help him get the eight thousand rupees due to him. This made Mohammad Shaffi angry who got Fateh Mohammad's whole family massacred. Militants also targeted relatives of political leaders in the district. In one such incident, on June 29, 1999, militants in the Arnas area of Reasi district killed Ali Mohammad Khan, the brother of Haji Buland Khan, an influential Gujjar leader.

Why the Gujjars Joined Militancy in Reasi

The involvement of the Gujjar community in militancy was never clear-cut and was the result of complex factors. When interviewed, some of the community headmen said that both sides – the security forces as well as the militants – suspected them (the Gujjars). At several places they had no alternative but to give shelter to militants otherwise their lives were threatened. The Gujjar community was perhaps one of the few Muslim communities of the region who dared to form VDCs to protect themselves against the militants. Owing to this, many Gujjars of the area became their victims. Since they could not get the protection of the security forces in the remote hilly areas, they joined the militants' ranks or provided indirect assistance. An additional reason cited by many locals was the lure of money given to those who worked as their guides. Of course, the religious factor cannot be ruled out altogether.

Militant Attacks on Hindus in Reasi

Militants also attacked Hindu majority areas in Reasi tehsil. Their aim was to keep the hills safe for their trek as well as to terrorize the population. As the area had a predominantly Hindu majority, they knew that local support would not be forthcoming. Therefore, they aimed to spread terror. In Reasi tehsil, barring the town, the population is scattered in the surrounding hills. Road connectivity in the tehsil is poor and many of the remote villages can only be accessed on foot, sometimes after walking for more than a day. Anticipating the danger, VDCs were constituted here in the late 1990s, and these became the militants' main targets.

On the night of April 17, 1998, militants slaughtered 28 Hindu villagers in Prankot village in the Reasi area. Prankote is an administrative unit comprising a group of villages of

Reasi. It can be reached only after an eight-hour trek over a mountainous stretch, the last motorable road being at a distance of eight kilometres. The news of the gruesome massacre reached the authorities after 10 hours and it took over 24 hours for the security forces to reach the village. The militants had hacked the villagers with cleavers; they had not used weapons.

The Prankot incident marked a new chapter in militancy in the state, when a series of mass killings of Hindus started. When

A nine-year-old child who was forcibly recruited by militants and finally rescued, demonstrating his skills in using an automatic weapon in Reasi district (Photograph by Luv Puri)

the electronic media reached the spot and beamed the pictures of 28 blood-splattered, beheaded bodies, it horrified the entire nation and sent shock waves throughout the hilly belt. Several families were completely wiped out in the attack. There were some lucky survivors. For instance Krishan Kumar lost his parents, two sisters and a younger brother. Twelve-year-old Sudesh lost her entire family that was massacred in front of her eyes. The incident provoked mass migrations with about 1,000 people from villages in Pauni and Reasi fleeing in terror, taking refuge in the safer areas of the district.

The VDCs could not provide adequate security cover to the population in the hilly areas of Reasi. The militants' superior weapons and poor backup from the security forces for the VDCs made them prone to high casualties. For instance, on April 8, 2002, militants struck at different houses in Dandli in groups of four, at 9 p.m. They opened fire indiscriminately and asked the VDC members to surrender their weapons and come out unarmed with their family members. The VDC members refused to give in and told the militants that they would rather fight to the last breath. In the nine-hour battle that ensued, seven people, including three children were killed. At 6 a.m. the next day, the first batch of the Special Operations Group of the J&K Police arrived at the spot, but by then the militants had escaped.

Other Areas Affected by Militancy

Udhampur district was also affected by militancy in the two areas of Dudu and Basantgarh. They lie in the Ram Nagar tehsil of this Hindu majority district. But in Dudu and Basantgarh, the Muslim population is high. Most of the Muslims belong to the Gujjar and Dogra communities. The two areas are located close to the southern areas of Doda district bordering Bhaderwah tehsil. These areas also border the hilly tract of Kathua district. Violence in the belt has been generally low due to the lack of response from the local population. The belt is sparsely populated and militants prefer to enter the safe zones of Doda district where they expect active response. The hills of the area fall along the militants 'highway' and VDCs were formed in anticipation of attacks on the vulnerable Hindu community in the hills. Occasionally, providing guns to the community in these remote interiors caused misgivings in the Muslim community. Militants took advantage of misgivings and cited them as reasons for attacking VDCs. A number of attacks took place in Dudu-Basantgarh like the one in 1999 summer when three VDC personnel were kidnapped and killed.

Kathua

Militancy entered Kathua during its last phase, where infiltrators from international border along Pathankot road joined militants from Doda or used the route to meet them in Doda. Kathua falls between the International Border and Doda district. Kathua's strategic importance, lies in the fact that it is the gateway to the state and borders the states of Punjab and Himachal Pradesh. In J&K it touches Jammu, Udhampur and the Doda districts of the Jammu region and most importantly also shares a 60-kilometre international border with Punjab province in Pakistan. The international border running along the district has a number of rivulets crossing it, which provide porous infiltration routes. Before militancy started, this border along the district, like the Jammu border, was used by smugglers.

Kathua is divided into two halves – the plains area and the hilly tract. The plains area comprising Kathua and Hiranagar tehsil touches Punjab state in India in the South-east. Most of the international border runs along Hiranagar tehsil, while a part of it runs along Kathua tehsil. As far as the community

Local women of Reasi district learn to use .303 rifles
(Photograph by Luv Puri)

Local men of Reasi district learn to use .303 rifles
(Photograph by Luv Puri)

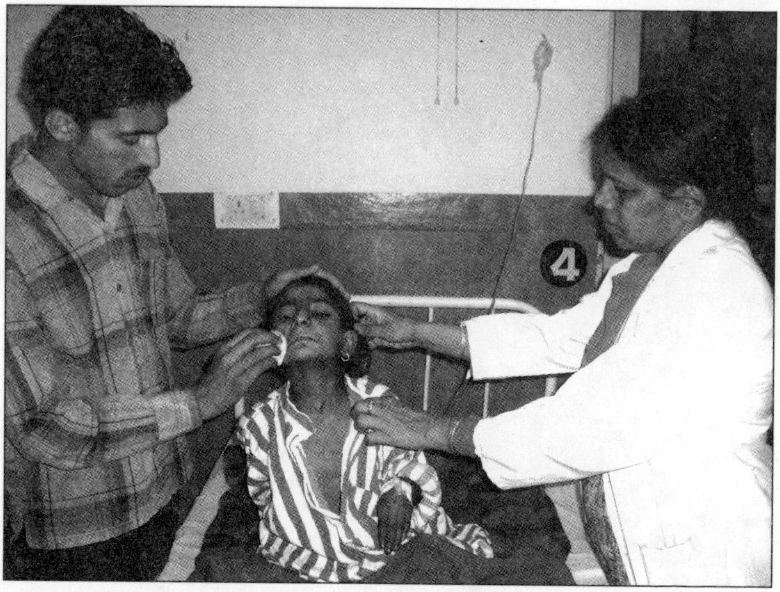

A Gujjar Muslim girl injured in a militant attack on her house (Photograph by Luv Puri)

profile is concerned, the Kathua plains have an overwhelming Hindu-majority, with the Muslim Gujjars scattered across the area. The northern areas of Basohli and Billawar tehsils are hilly, and inhabited mostly by Muslims comprising Gujjars, Dogras and the Kashmiri speaking communities. Most of the Kashmiri-speaking Muslims live in Lohai Malhar. The blocks of Bani and Lohai Malhar, situated in Basohli and Billawar tehsils respectively, are a vast hilly tract. These blocks have a heterogeneous profile, with sizeable numbers of both the Hindu and Muslim communities.

Militancy in Kathua

Militants use the 60-kilometre stretch of the international border to infiltrate into J&K from Pakistan, and whenever there is

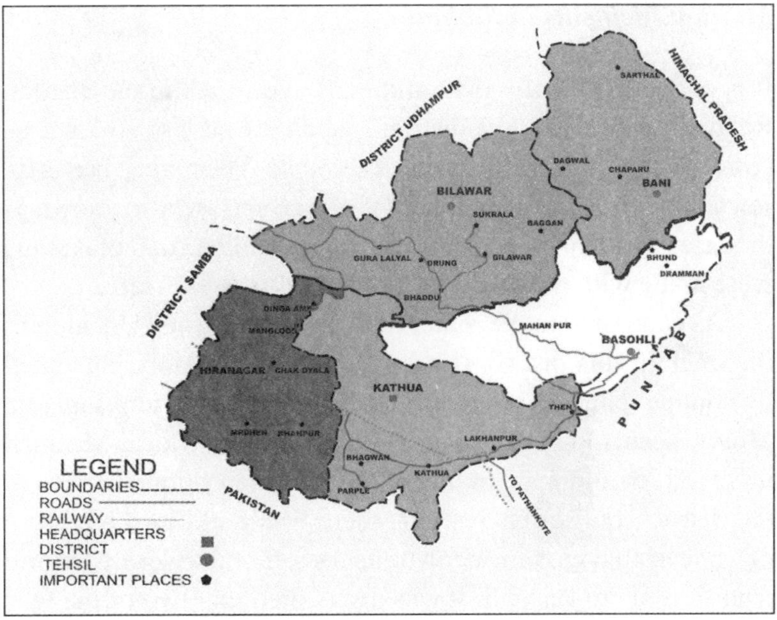

Map of Kathua district

pressure on the militants in Doda, they enter Kathua for refuge. During the turmoil in Punjab state, when the border along Punjab was fenced, Sikh militants started using the international border to enter J&K and then gain entry into neighbouring Punjab for their operations. After the end of the Punjab militancy, Kashmiri militants also started using the international border to gain entry into the state and venture further into Doda district. The hilly tract of the district is sparsely populated and in order to ensure the safety of civilians, VDCs were formed both in the plains and the hilly tracts. The important Jammu-Pathankot National Highway No. 1A, as well as the railway track pass through the district. In the past, several attempts were made to damage the railway track. VDCs formed in the plains have also been entrusted with the responsibility of protecting the track.

Militant Incidents in Kathua

It is only occasionally that militants have struck in the district. Relatively speaking, the district has witnessed less violence as compared to the other districts of the state. The plains, barring a few incidents, have been free of violence and are also known as the safest parts of the state. Strikes in the hilly terrain of Kathua were made with the aim of keeping the 'highway' safe.

As compared to the routes in Rajouri, Reasi and Udhampur, the track in this district is used less, as it is mainly populated by Hindus. The response from the Muslim population is mixed. Money seems to be the main motivation for the local Muslims involved in militancy. In one of the more sensational strikes in the district, on March 1, 2001, there was a bid to rob a crore of rupees that government treasury officials were carrying from Kathua to Basohli. It was discovered that two of the four militants, namely Zahoor Hussain and Muzaffar, belonged to Basohli in Kathua district. Militants have also struck in the areas near the neighbouring Doda district. On April 5, 2001, a group of militants barged into the house of a BJP leader, Abdul Ghani Bhat, and killed him and his relatives. They also killed a retired forest guard in the Lohai Malhar area of Billawar tehsil. They entered Abdul Ghani Bhat's house, to eliminate two of his close relatives who had given up militancy. Militants active in this part have also struck in the neighbouring areas of Punjab. For instance, in December 2001, they struck the Mamoon Army camp in Pathankot. There have been occasional incidents in the plains as well. Two brothers were killed near the border in village Ghati, while hunting in the forests. Apparently the militants killed them because they had been spotted by the former.

The only vital link between the state and the rest of the country, the Jammu-Pathankot National Highway was once also a scene of a militant strike. On October 1, 2002, the day of the J&K elections, two fidayeens, crossed the international border at Hiranagar, and dressed in police uniforms, hijacked a bus at a place called Katar. They directed the driver to take them to the election booth in the town. The driver after some distance rammed the bus on the right side of the road when it was a few metres away from the Jammu-Pathankot National Highway. The militants came out of the bus in panic and started firing indiscriminately, whereby seven people lost their lives. They managed to escape from the spot. The security forces after a massive hunt succeeded in finding the militants after the police intercepted some messages between the latter and their mentors in Shakergarh tehsil of Pakistan. On October 3, 2002, the Jammu Police tracked them down in the Jandi Nala area of Hiranagar, three kilometres from the Jammu-Pathankot National Highway. Both militants were gunned down in the encounter and one police officer, Deputy Superintendent of Police, Jagtar Singh, also lost his life. According to the police, both belonged to Punjab province in Pakistan. The local people say that they have spotted militants several times, as they make their way through the area.

Involvement of the Local Population in Militancy in Kathua

Most of the Muslim population is concentrated in the hilly stretch of the district with a scattering of Muslim Gujjars living in the plains. The militants 'highway' to enter Doda district passes through this area. It is a long journey, taking three to four days, and hence shelter and information about the paths are essential. The army does not have prominent presence in the remote interior parts of the hilly tract and militants are able to get shelter at the point of a gun. Sometimes the Muslim Gujjar community has shown bravery, providing vital clues to the security forces, leading to success in anti-militancy operations. For instance in 2001, in Village Digam in Billawar tehsil, Gujjars tipped off the security forces about the presence of militants in their dhoks (temporary shelter) leading to the killing of seven of them. The hilly areas of the district are some of the poorest areas of the state and the lure of money given by militants helped them in getting local support. The militants need the support of Gujjars and Bakerwals for their movements. Gujjars and Bakerwals are scattered across the district. While the Gujjars know all the routes in the district, the Bakerwals are familiar with the inter-district routes. Hence, they can provide vital information to the militants that can make latter's mobility in the area much easier.

Notes

1. The Dogra hero, Mian Deedo, put up a stiff resistance against Maharaja Ranjit Singh from 1812 to 1820. The Dogra patriot fought against the occupation of the state by the Maharaja. He was shot dead by Raja Gulab Singh's men at Sanjhi Chhat near Mata Vaishnodevi's shrine, while he was offering prayers to the Goddess.
2. Gulab Singh signed the Treaty of Amritsar with the British on March 16, 1846. The treaty brought together the various kingdoms into a single political entity called the State of Jammu and Kashmir.
3. Prior to 2006, Reasi district was part of Udhampur district.

5

Militancy Strikes the Winter Capital

Jammu district is by far the most important and populous district of J&K, and Jammu city is the winter capital of the state for six months. As the district is geographically a plains area, it has a well-connected road network linking it to other districts of Jammu and Kashmir. Apart from being the Headquarters of the state government departments, during the winter, Jammu city is also the Headquarters of the regional offices.[1] It is the main scene of political activity in Jammu region and the mood prevailing here is in many ways representative of the rest of Jammu district. The additional factor for this being that the city and the district are culturally much less diverse than the other districts of the region. Jammu district has an overwhelmingly Hindu majority of 91 per cent, with Muslims constituting only 4 per cent of its population (Census 1981). The others are Sikhs and Christians. A majority of the Muslim population in the city is concentrated in the peripheral areas and comprises 4.27 per cent of the total population. Most of the Muslims in rural areas belong to the Gujjar community (who are Muslims throughout the state) and are the main providers of dairy products to the city. Though Dogri is the predominant mother tongue of the people, its close linguistic cousins, Punjabi, Pahari and Gojri, are also spoken in the district.

To understand the current reaction to militancy, it is important to study the past history of the region. Before the

Partition, Muslims constituted a little less than 50 per cent of the Hindu population in Jammu district. According to the 1941 Census, the Muslims totalled 1,70,789 and the Hindus, 2,48,173 persons. The district, particularly the city, was one of the areas of the country that was worst affected by communal carnage, in which many Muslims were killed by Hindu mobs resulting in large-scale migration of Muslims to the neighbouring areas of West Punjab in Pakistan. Prior to the Partition, several localities such as Ustad Mohalla, Afghan Mohalla, Jullahka Mohalla, Peer Mitha, Lakhdata and Rajinder Bazaar were mainly Muslim dominated, but the city was in no way communally polarized, as both Muslims and Hindus lived in large numbers in the same localities. The two communities shared several common features. In the sphere of devotion, the Pirs and Sufis were common to both. Even today, the city has several Ziarats of Muslim saints to which Hindus and Muslims show equal devotion. The outflow of Muslims from the district during the Partition, and at the same time, the inflow of a large number of Hindus and Sikhs from Pakistan-administered Jammu and Kashmir cast a shadow on the reactions of the populace to the various events that occurred in the state. The entire social and cultural composition was altered as populations running into lakhs from various parts of Pakistan-administered Jammu and Kashmir namely, Mirpur, Kotli, Muzaffarabad, Bhimber, Poonch and parts of neighbouring Sialkot district settled in Jammu district.

The agony and the circumstances under which they left their homes have to an extent influenced the reactions of the people, including the younger generations, to current events. Jammu district's involvement with militancy has been both direct and indirect. The indirect involvement has been immense since the flow of information to and from the other districts in Jammu region is swift, and the city reacts immediately, with

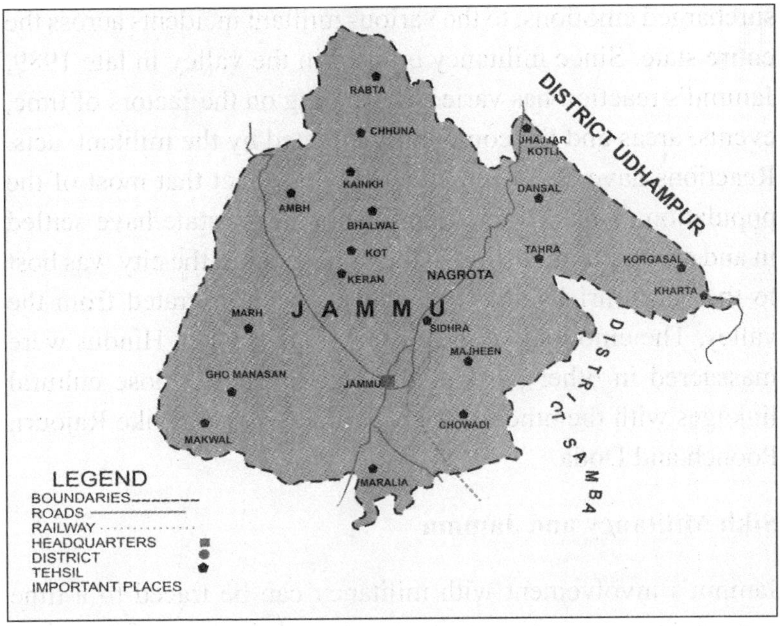

Map of Jammu tehsil

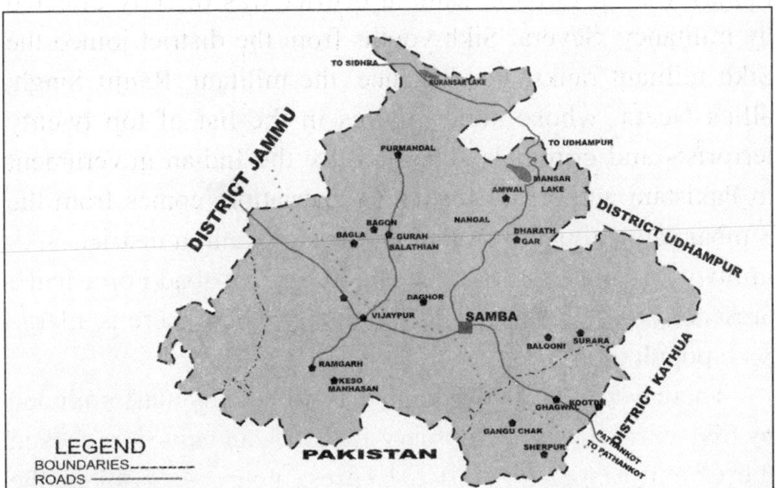

Samba district (Before 2006, Samba was part of Jammu district)

surcharged emotions, to the various militant incidents across the entire state. Since militancy erupted in the valley in late 1989, Jammu's reaction has varied, depending on the factors of time, events, areas and the community affected by the militant acts. Reactions have also been affected by the fact that most of the population displaced due to militancy in the state have settled in and around Jammu city. In the initial stages, the city was host to the Kashmiri Pandit community, which migrated from the valley. The emotions of the city ran higher when Hindus were massacred in other parts of the region, due to close cultural linkages with the other districts particularly areas like Rajouri, Poonch and Doda.

Sikh Militancy and Jammu

Jammu's involvement with militancy can be traced to a time even before Kashmiri militancy started. In the 1980s, when Punjab was in turmoil, Jammu district was directly affected by militancy. Several Sikh youths from the district joined the Sikh militant ranks. For instance, the militant, Ranjit Singh, allias Neeta, whose name figures in the list of top twenty terrorists and criminals submitted by the Indian government to Pakistani authorities for their repatriation, comes from the Simbal camp situated on the outskirts of Jammu district. Sikh militant organizations like the Khalistan Zindabad Force had a presence on the outskirts of Jammu city where there is a large Sikh population.

There were occasional bomb blasts allegedly masterminded by Sikh extremists. On February 13, 1985, an explosion rocked the Calcutta-bound Sealdah Express near Ghagwal in the neighbouring Kathua district, in which 12 passengers were killed and one bogey was completely destroyed. A number of Sikh militants were shot dead in different encounters in the district.

There were ugly reprisals by Sikh militants against people who left their ranks. In one such broad daylight attack in the early 1990s, a former militant, Avtar Singh, was shot dead allegedly by Kashmiri militants in the Nanak Nagar area of the city, since Kashmiri as well as Sikh militants suspected him of being an informer. The city also witnessed one of the worst anti-Sikh riots on January 13, 1989 in which 15 Sikhs were killed and several injured. But over a period of time the Hindu-Sikh tensions subsided as normalcy was restored in Punjab. The security of the district was once again threatened with the militancy that was starting in Kashmir.

Susceptibility of Jammu City to Militancy

There are a number of factors that make the city a soft target for militants. The district shares an approximately 198-kilometre international border with Pakistan. From the Ravi river to Mannawar Tawi, the international border has a terrain that provides several infiltration routes.[2] Jammu city is just ten kilometres from the international border. Before militancy started in the state, the international border was used for smuggling. Taking advantage of several ravines and ditches, the smugglers would sneak into Pakistan and return. The main route taken by the infiltrators was the Basantar corridor in Samba and the Hiranagar sector of Kathua district, which again has a number of ravines and ditches.

There is linguistic affinity between the people on both sides of the border, more specifically with the Sialkot sector in Pakistan. Thus, it was difficult to detect smugglers from either side by the authorities in India and Pakistan. In the pre-Partition era, the Jammu-Sialkot relationship was very close and Sialkot district in Pakistan was linked to the rest of the country through Jammu by rail. In the later years of militancy, the militants also started crossing the international border, using its porous patches to infiltrate into the region. In the initial period, the militants first infiltrated into Jammu district from where they started their long trek to Doda through Lake Mansar and parts of Kathua district.

Village Defence Groups were formed in Jammu along the international border in October 1995 as a self-defence mechanism. On several occasions, VDGs encountered militants and informed the security forces, thereby giving the forces adequate time to arrive where they were spotted. For instance, in August 2001 in the Sapwal area, VDGs discovered a plot by the militants to sabotage a railway track, which was thwarted by the joint efforts of the army and VDGs.

Major Strikes in Jammu

The first time the militants carried out a murderous assault in the city was on March 19, 1994. The attack was on the former Speaker of the J&K Legislative Assembly, Wali Mohammed Itoo. He was gunned down in Jammu as he came out of a mosque in the Talab Khatikan locality. The very fact that the militants could carry out such an open attack with precision shocked the people of the city. Just months later, on June 16, 1994, a powerful blast rocked a minibus in Jammu city leaving seven people dead. On November 22, 1994, there was a similar bus blast in the city in which nine people were killed and 36 injured. A few days later on December 12, in yet another blast in a passenger bus near Jammu, three people, including a woman, were killed and 10 others injured.

The year 1995 was no different. On January 26, 1995, the then Governor, K.V. Krishna Rao, escaped a bid on his life when three bombs went off in the M.A.M. Stadium in Jammu; eight people were killed, including three officials from the

Information Department, and 45 were injured. K.V. Krishna Rao was delivering his customary speech on Republic Day when one of the bombs exploded only a few yards away from him. The incident shook the entire nation. The very fact that militants could carry out such an act against the Head of the State in one of the most guarded and sanitized areas on the occasion of Republic Day caused ripples within security circles. In the middle of the year, on July 20, 1995, another blast rocked the heart of the city in the Purani Mandi area in which 19 people were killed and 60 injured.

After militancy moved to the Jammu plains, militants also targeted the railway track,which at places is situated only a few kilometers from the international border. There were some unsuccessful attempts earlier as well. On January 21, 1990, for example, there was a blast a few metres from the railway station near the Food Corporation of India (FCI) godown. One bogey of a stationary goods train was damaged. Eight passengers were killed on June 24, 1999, when a blast rocked the Delhi-bound Shalimar Express near Bari Brahamna; a bomb was planted on the track. Similarly on February 10, 2000, five passengers of the Calcutta-bound Sealdah Express were killed and eight injured in a blast.

Suicide Attacks in the City

The first suicide attack in the city took place on August 1, 2000, in which pilgrims to the holy Amarnath cave in Kashmir were the targets. The militants attacked the heavily guarded office in Jammu city where the Amarnath-bound pilgrims were registered. A watershed in the character of militancy in the state was the suicide attack on the Railway Station on the evening of August 7, 2001. Nine people, including two army men, two women and two sadhus were killed and 30 others injured, some of them seriously. It was believed to be the handiwork of three militants. One militant was killed, while the others managed to flee in the melee that followed. It was the first suicide attack in Jammu city, which resulted in such large-scale killings, and it increased the sense of insecurity among the citizens, from which they are yet to recover. During the next year, 2002, a series of suicide attacks hit the city and its periphery at regular intervals.

On March 30, 2002, two militants launched a suicide attack on the historic Raghunath Temple situated in the heart of Jammu city. Both militants were killed but not before they killed seven people, including three security personnel – the death toll later rose to nine. In another incident on May 14, 2002, three militants launched a suicide attack on an army family camp. The modus operandi was notable. Three militants, dressed in army combat uniforms boarded a Jammu-bound bus coming from Kulu in Himachal Pradesh, at Samba, 40 kilometres from Jammu city in the early morning hours. Just as the bus reached Kaluchak Army Camp, at around 5.35 a.m., the terrorists forced the driver to stop and started firing indiscriminately on the passengers. Seven people, including four men and three women, were killed on the spot. Thereafter, the militants ran towards the camp of the 196 Artillery Unit of the Army, scaled the walls and entered the family quarters. Twenty-three people died in the attack, including ten children, eight women and five army men. The militants were killed only after five hours at around 10.30 a.m., when commandos equipped with rocket launchers were pressed into action. The incident provoked an outrage in the country and led to mass deployment of forces on the borders. The threat of war between India and Pakistan loomed large. There was evidence to show that the attackers had come from the bordering Sialkot district of Pakistan, as a cinema ticket of a Sialkot cinema hall was found in the possession of the militants.

Only two months later, on the evening of July 13, 2002, there was a similar suicide attack. This time the militants targeted Rajiv Nagar slum area situated on the periphery of the Jammu city. Two men in their late teens arrived in the evening and started firing indiscriminately on the slum dwellers. They managed to escape after firing for half an hour. In this incident, twenty-nine people, including a large number of children were killed. A few days after the incident, on August 2, the Jammu police managed to eliminate one of the militants; and some days later the other militant, identified as Mohammad Abdullah, from Pakistan, was apprehended in the neighbouring dense forests. In the operation three police personnel were killed.

Towards the end of the year, on November 24, 2002, militants launched yet another attack in the evening hours, on Raghunath Temple and a neighbouring Shivalaya temple. One militant was killed in Raghunath Temple that evening while the other the next day. In this attack, 12 people died. On June 28, 2003 in a pre-dawn attack, two fidayeens pierced the heavily guarded Sanjuwan Army Camp and killed 12 sleeping army personnel. Later both of them were killed. About a month later on the evening of July 21, 2003, militants struck the base camp to the Vaishno Devi Shrine in the Katra area of Reasi district. Two grenades were lobbed at the Vaishno Devi pilgrims whereby six pilgrims, including an infant, died and more than 40 people were injured.

Hours later, on July 22, 2003, in a sensational attack, suicide bombers almost succeeded in wiping out the entire top leadership of the Northern Army Command at Tanda Army Camp situated near Akhnoor town, 24 kilometres from Jammu city. Early in the morning, three militants sneaked into the Tanda EME camp (repair workshop) and killed seven jawans. Two militants were killed and in the evening, when the GOC Northern Command,

Lt. Gen. Hari Prasad, the 16 Corps Commander, Lt. Gen. T.P.S. Brar, along with other senior commanders came to inspect the area, a militant appeared from under the bushes and blew himself up to target the commanders. The commanders escaped unhurt but a Brigadier was killed in the incident and a Major General was seriously injured. There was another suicide attack on January 2, 2004, in which four security personnel were killed along with both the suicide attackers. A similar attack on the pattern of Kaluchak suicide attack was attempted on 10th May, 2008. A group of militants who had entered through Sialkot area via international border tried to attack family quarters of army personnel in Samba town. The militants were spotted just before they were about to attack. Though militants were killed after 24 hours of operation, six persons also died as militants had forced their way into nearby civilian residential area.

The Background of Militants Activity in Jammu Plains

Militants did not expect to get support in Jammu plains. As such, they chose soft targets. In the 1990s, they exploded bombs in crowded places or in passenger buses. In the recent past, they carried out more sensational acts like suicide attacks on temples and other crowded places. The aim clearly was to provoke the Hindu population and attract publicity. In most of these attacks, no militant organization claimed responsibility. While the police described the suicide attacks as the handiwork of the Lashkar-e-Toiba outfit, the commonality in the attackers' place of origin was conspicuous. They all came from the Punjab province in Pakistan, a region which broadly shares similar culture with the Jammu plains. Kashmiri-speaking militants have not been involved in suicide attacks. Owing to the similarity in language, the militants from across the border cannot be easily identified as they are indistinguishable from the local population in Jammu district, whereas Kashmiri-speaking militants do not enjoy this advantage.

Most of the attackers who carried out the sensational terrorists acts in the city in the recent past, crossed the international border from Punjab province in Pakistan. For instance, in the Rajiv Nagar attack, the militant who was arrested some days later identified himself as Mohammad Abdullah, a resident of Multan in Punjab and spoke chaste Punjabi during his brief interaction with the press. Even in other incidents where attackers have been shot dead, the police in most cases have discovered their origin to be Punjab province in Pakistan.

The Effects of Militancy on Society

In the last decade, militancy has seriously affected society in the district, particularly in Jammu city. Several families in the city come from different parts of the region and sometimes maintain close linkages with their respective districts of origin. Both Hindus and Muslims from as far as the Bhaderwah area of Doda district and Kishtwar district have settled in Jammu region. Militancy in their respective areas of origin did have an impact on the people. For instance the Muslim youth from Doda who grew up and was educated in Jammu pioneered the armed movements in their respective areas. Similarly, when the series of massacres against Hindus rocked Doda, it led to a surcharged reaction from the Hindus from that district living in Jammu city. Direct involvement in militancy by the local Muslims of the district has not been proved till date, though there are a few exceptions. There were also a few instances of bravery by local Muslims who provided vital information to the security forces, even at the risk to their lives. For instance, Kaka, a Gujjar Muslim and resident of the Raika forests, near Rajiv Nagar, at high risk to his life, overpowered the terrorist involved in the Rajiv Nagar incident when the latter came to his house for shelter. Kaka called the police and handed him over.

Militancy acquired a new character in the state when it entered the province in the hilly districts of the region, where Hindus had settled and were soft targets. Both Hindus and Muslims living in the city have their own insecurities. The reaction to the various massacres of Hindus, in places where they are in a majority has at times acquired communal overtones causing insecurity among the minuscule Muslim population living in ghettoized areas. The BJP's demands after every massacre, that Muslim localities should be sanitized and searched, have only enhanced this insecurity.

Notes

1. The capital of the state of Jammu and Kashmir shifts biannually from Jammu to Srinagar with the onset of summer and vice-versa with the onset of winter.
2. From the Ravi river to Mannawar Tawi, the area touching Sialkot district in Pakistan, is called the Indo-Pakistan International Border.

6

Conclusion

Counter-terror Strategies for Jammu Region

In the earlier sections, the various factors that led to the rise of militancy in Jammu region have been detailed. This chapter will identify the peculiarities of militancy in Jammu region in relation to that of Kashmir. The start of militancy and its spread in Jammu region caused a decisive shift in its character, composition and objectives. It coincided with the changing attitude of the world to militant movements post 9/11. In the early 1990s, J&K militancy was generally viewed as a freedom struggle by the Kashmiris. Now it came to be branded as terrorism. The mindless killing of innocents, which was the pronounced feature of the Jammu phase of militancy, brought a qualitative change in the world's perception. While the world reacted quite strongly to the violations of Human Rights by the security forces in the early 1990s in the Kashmir valley, the condemnation against the killing of innocents by militants was also instantaneous. The principle of using violence as an instrument for settling the Kashmir dispute no longer finds many supporters in the world.

Militancy in Jammu, from its inception, was quite different in several ways from that in the Kashmir region. It was a mix of religious extremism, ethnic antagonism and, at times, criminalization. Even from the perspective of the militant outfits, different strategies were adopted in fighting the security personnel. Gauging the necessity of different tactics for the Jammu region some militant outfits formed different sub-outfits. For instance, the largest indigenous militant group still active in the state, Hizbul Mujahideen, set up a different sub-group called the Hizbul Mujahideen Pir-Panjal Regiment for this side of the state. The outfit had its own commanders who planned their strategies. By targeting the Hindus in the hills and the Muslims who were suspected as informers, the militants wanted to establish their superiority in the interior areas. The hills surrounding the roads also gave them an advantage. Safeguarding the road network is still one of the most difficult tasks for the security agencies, particularly in the Rajouri-Poonch tract and to the north of Reasi, that is the Mahore-Arnas belt.

The complex factors in each district of Jammu, which were responsible for the growth of militancy, have been described in the previous chapters. With the apparent difference in the character of terrorism, strategies adopted in the Kashmir valley did not work in Jammu region. The reasons are obvious – a different terrain and a totally different composition of society. Therefore, even counter-terror strategies for the region had to be different and devised according to ground realities. The factors of terrain, societal composition and the political framework in the region, all demanded a different approach. Unlike Kashmir, where the terrain consists of plains and a road network has been built, the transportation system in Jammu region is underdeveloped. Even today, several villages of the region can only be accessed after trekking for over a day, and this underlines the difficulties involved in counter-terror strategies. This is the reason why most of the time security agencies have failed to track down militants who committed gruesome massacres. At times, the only way to evacuate the injured is with the help of helicopters. With the exception of Jammu district all the other districts are hilly. Even connectivity within the districts is poor. The Herculean task of providing security to the vulnerable population requires in-depth studies. As militancy in Jammu started at different times in different areas and each had its own characteristics, each district requires a different approach, but at the same time, good quality coordination within the region and between the agencies in Kashmir is equally important.

The success of counter-terror strategies in Jammu will have an impact on the militancy movement in Kashmir as well. The region provides one of the safest infiltration routes for the militants to enter the state, (including the Kashmir valley), for their activities in the hilly areas of Jammu and strikes in the plains. Lessons must be learnt from past experience, including that of the 1965 war, when the collapse and many a times the absence of cooperation and coordination between security forces, the civil administration and the political leadership handicapped the role of the security forces and facilitated the infiltrator's task of controlling large parts of Rajouri and Poonch. With its vast terrain, the region provided innumerable escape routes to the militants. As most of the Indian military presence in counter-militancy operations was limited to the Kashmir valley, militants used Jammu as a safe shelter in the earlier stages.

When local recruits joined militants it acquired a new impetus. Thus, started the fight between the security forces and militants for domination of the hilly areas of Jammu. Reaching every corner of the district is an impossible task for the forces. The militants merge with the population in the towns and strike at will. The region's communally sensitive history, with Muslims and Hindus both living in large numbers in the state, provides a fertile ground for the protagonists of a pan-Islamic movement in Jammu and Kashmir.

The areas where there were early recruitments had a background of communally sensitive incidents. For instance, Bhaderwah tehsil is one of the most communally sensitive parts of the state and has a history of riots over petty issues. This communally fragile environment worsened with the violence in the state. A section of Muslims were sympathetic to the militant movement and the sphere and degree of sympathy widened with the excesses of the security forces. On the other hand, Hindus considered the army as their saviours and treated Muslims with suspicion. The extremists in both communities were able to widen the gulf even further.

Reduction of Militancy in Jammu Region

The reduction of militancy in Jammu region was faster than in the Kashmir valley. This demonstrates that the causes of the rise and decline of militancy were quite different from those in the Valley. After the J&K Legislative Assembly Elections in 2002, conditions in Jammu, in particular its communal situation, improved. Further, various ethnic groups felt relatively empowered with the shaping up of Jammu's political identity. This was due to the fact that Jammu's political weight was greatly enhanced in the state of Jammu and Kashmir after the 2002 Legislative Elections. The Gujjar community started rebelling against militants, most prominently in the Marrah area of the Surankote belt of Poonch district. Operation Sarp Vinash in April 2003, one of the largest counter-militancy operations in Jammu and Kashmir, was principally carried out by the local Gujjars who liberated the area from the militants' control. The revolt was led initially by Gojri-speaking Muslims against the extremism of the Punjabi-speaking militants from across the Line of Control. Militancy declined in Doda and Kishtwar districts when Ghulam Nabi Azad, a local person, was projected by the

Congress Party as its Chief Ministerial candidate, and became a secular symbol of a once bitterly divided society. This was amply demonstrated when Azad won the election from his native assembly constituency of Bhaderwah, a communally sensitive

Local Gujjar men fight against militancy in Poonch district (Photograph by special arrangement)

area with Hindus and Muslims in almost equal numbers. The situation had invariably worsened in Bhaderwah after the outbreak of militancy. Azad won by a record margin of about 58,000 votes against his nearest rival, the BJP's Dhanatar Singh, thanks to support from both the Hindus and the Muslims. Azad got 62,072 votes against Singh's 4,057 in the eight rounds of counting. There was a qualitative shift in the politics of Jammu when Azad became the Chief Minister of the state in November 2005. This was part of an agreement between the coalition partners — the Congress Party and the PDP — to rotate the post. All communities of the region discovered a common symbol of their pride, when for the first time since 1947, a Jammu leader became the head of government of the state. Thereafter, militancy lost its raison d'être in the region.

The Peace Process

The peace process between India and Pakistan also led to the opening of points along the Line of Control for civilian traffic,

Surrender ceremony of militants (Photograph: Courtesy Ministry of Defence)

Surrender ceremony of militants (Photograph: Courtesy Ministry of Defence)

Relatives gather on either side of the LoC after the decision by the Indian and Pakistani governments to open LoC points for civilian traffic (Photograph by Luv Puri)

A view of Pakistani troops along the LoC adjoining Poonch district (Photograph by Luv Puri)

mainly for members of divided families. The main beneficiaries were Muslim families living in Jammu region. It is they who suffered the brunt of the division of Jammu and Kashmir. Most of the people who came from Pakistan-administered Jammu and Kashmir visited different parts of Jammu where their relatives resided. The civilian traffic at the LoC to the south of the Pir Panjal range is much larger than that in the Kashmir valley.[1] When the much-hyped Srinagar-Muzaffarabad bus was started it was believed that it would unite many divided families of the state.[2] On the contrary, it was the Chakan da Bagh and Tattapani route in Jammu region that united more families ever since these points were opened for civilian traffic.

There were other long-term spin-offs with the opening of the LoC. Many residents from Pakistan-administered Jammu and Kashmir, who came across the LoC became privy to the fact that there were no restrictions imposed on Muslims in the Indian

Pakistan-administered Jammu and Kashmir residents being tear-gassed by Pakistani troops as they forcibly tried to cross over the LoC to meet their relatives on the Indian side of Jammu and Kashmir. The incident occurred on November 7, 2005 when India sent relief material to Pakistan-administered Jammu and Kashmir after the October 8, 2005 earthquake. (Photograph by Luv Puri)

state, and that they were treated at a par with other religious communities. This went a long way in negating the propaganda by extremist militant outfits in Pakistan and Pakistan-administered Jammu and Kashmir who often claimed that Muslims were discriminated against in the Muslim majority J&K, particularly in the Hindu-dominated Jammu region. Several militants arrested from extremist outfits like the Lashkar, belonging to Punjab province in Pakistan and to Pakistan-administered Jammu and Kashmir have stated that they primarily joined militancy because of religious indoctrination. They were drawn to militancy after hearing that Muslims in Jammu and Kashmir were persecuted by the state machinery. Punjabi-speaking Mohammad Abdullah, the youth who carried out the attack on the slum dwellers in Rajiv Nagar on July 14, 2002, stated after his arrest in a talk with the author that he was swayed by the Lashkar's propaganda that the Muslims of Jammu were getting a rough deal from the state machinery and the Indian army. The warm reception that the Muslims from across the LoC received from co-linguist Hindus and Sikhs on this side of the border, which was reciprocated when some Hindus visited the other side, had a salutary impact on inter-communal relations in the region.

The Long-Term Solution

Jammu may have become a relatively peaceful zone after a decade of violence that resulted in communal and ethnic fissures in its composite society. The situation may have reversed but that does not mean that a permanent solution has been found tackling its complex problems, which have a direct impact on the state as a whole. As an empowered political entity, further improvements in Jammu can go a long way in the evolution of a harmonious and federal state of Jammu and Kashmir. Personalities cannot substitute political, economic and social institutions. Institutions are extremely important as they provide an effective and long-standing solution to the urge for power among the people of the different regions of the state. The present highly centralized polity in Jammu and Kashmir without any decentralized structure is least capable of accommodating the urges and aspirations of every ethnic group, region and religion.

Apart from constructing an effective security strategy to block infiltration at the frontiers of the borders, the people's support and cooperation with the security forces is essential. Militants need local support to operate in the area, for shelter and to act as guides for paths into the interior. No strategy can work until the people are involved in counter-terror activities. The role of an active police force is pivotal and, therefore, local recruitment to the police forces needs to be encouraged. An efficient police force with a good information network is very effective for counter-terror operations.

Human Rights Institutions

In the Muslim belt of the Jammu region mass anti-India demonstrations or those for independence have been rare. However, such demonstrations do occur when the security forces kill an innocent person. Incidents like these further weaken the struggle against terror. The forces need to be sensitized to the importance of winning the confidence of the local people and must be made accountable for their lapses. Several Human Rights Groups and media representatives are based in Srinagar. There is a need for the State Human Rights Commission to open offices in this part of the state to monitor and check Human Rights abuses. The office in Jammu lacks staff and is perpetually locked.[3] The security of the population in the remote hills spread over long distances needs special attention. Usually the militants strike at places that fall along the highway routes to ensure that their path is safe. The population scattered in the interiors of Jammu region are vulnerable and have to be protected.

In the plains of Jammu region, the security strategy depends on strengthening the intelligence network. As mentioned earlier, it is far easier for a militant coming from Pakistan-administered Jammu and Kashmir or Punjab province to carry out an attack in Jammu, given the shared linguistic and cultural commonality with the local populace. Almost all militant strikes in Jammu city are the handiwork of Punjabi speaking militants. However, it is a great irony that the security agencies' main thrust has been to keep an eye on the Kashmiri speaking youth. A Punjabi-speaking youth from Pakistan can intermingle and adjust with the people of Jammu city far more easily than a Kashmiri youth. This basic fact has to be understood by the security agencies. It is essential to develop a good security and intelligence network in the interior areas of the city. This is equally true for the police forces. Dynamic officers should be posted in the region – personnel who can handle local complex situations and are able to engage in regular interactions with the people in the border villages.

Civil Administration

The civil administration in the area has failed to meet the changing needs of the people of Jammu region. Government servants regard posting in the hilly belt of the region as punishment posting and, therefore, lack the will to perform, with some exceptions. The centralized polity of the state with decisions-making powers concentrated alternately in the twin capital cities of Srinagar and Jammu every six months is responsible for the lack of morale and initiative of the local administration. The locals allege that as soon as militancy started, there was a vacuum in the civil administration in the hilly areas of Jammu region. Security agencies took over civil administrative duties and this

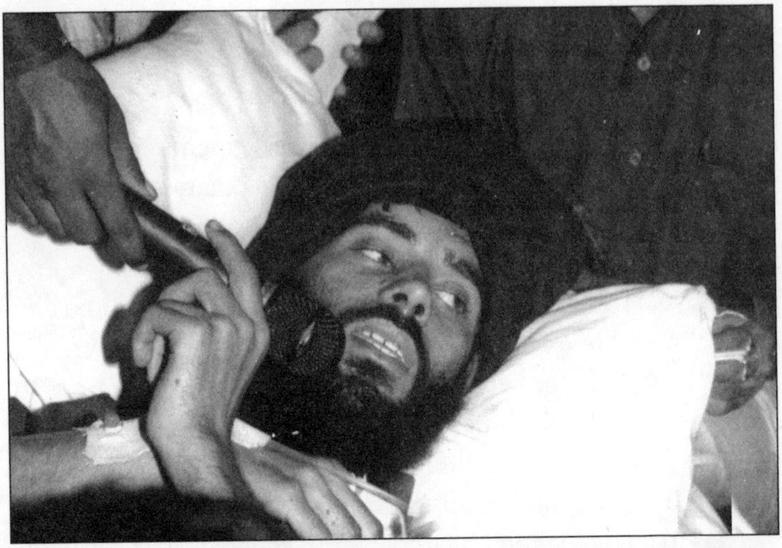

Punjabi-speaking Mohammad Shahzad, District Commander Laskhar-e-Toiba, a militant (belonging to Pakistan) apprehended by Indian troops (Photograph: Courtesy Ministry of Defence)

continues even today. After the imposition of the Disturbed Area Act in Jammu region in August 2001, the civil administration was further paralysed as the army was entrusted with additional powers. For instance, it tried to manage schools located in the militancy affected areas. With due respect to the army, it would have performed a better service to the people of the district if it had merely helped the civil administration to function effectively rather than trying to replace its functions. As an example, the absence of the civil authority resulted in teachers playing truant even if there was no real militant threat. Much of the teachers' time is spent in trying to get themselves transferred to their home districts. The policy should be such that the lower layers of the administration should be manned by native residents of the area, with obvious exceptions. At the higher levels, employees who understand the complexities existing in the district should be deputed or at least, made to learn about these. In the interior areas, the civil administration can become operational with the active support of security agencies and decentralized elected bodies. Energetic bureaucrats ought to be assigned the task of handling the border districts and suitable incentives should be given to them.

The communally disturbed parts of Rajouri, Doda and Kishtwar districts need delicate handling. The population in Rajouri, Doda and Kishtwar is religiously heterogeneous, and the chasm between the Hindus and Muslims still exists. Some political elements have been quick to exploit the insecurities of both communities. Any massacre of Hindus in the interiors of Rajouri, Kishtwar and Doda invariably leads to a violent reaction elsewhere in the region. Similarly, the killing of an innocent Muslim leads to a violent response by the Muslims of the surrounding area. The civil administration, security agencies, political parties, and civil society have to coordinate their actions so that such incidents do not occur.

The Cultural Component of the Anti-Terror Strategy

Mass media can go a long way in tackling propaganda from the other side and creating emotional integration of the border districts with the rest of the country. An overdose of religion in Pakistan-administered Jammu and Kashmir, especially in the last two decades, has led to cultural starvation. Programmes based on the rich cultural heritage of the area should be telecast. Special attention should be given to revive folk music and literary programmes. This can be used as a cultural offensive by India towards the people living in Pakistan-administered Jammu and Kashmir, as the programmes could appeal to prospective recruits to militant outfits in that area. The success of the cultural component in the anti-terror strategy can be illustrated by an incident that occurred a few years ago. In November 2001, militants belonging to Pakistan-administered Jammu and Kashmir kidnapped a Hindu teacher. After roaming around for days in the forest under militant captivity, one day the teacher started singing some lyrics from the *Saifulmalok*, a famous epic of the region. The lyrics melted the militants' hearts. They became friendly with the teacher and let him go. This incident portrays the significant potential of the common cultural heritage.

The border belt has a proud history of communal harmony with Muslims, Hindus and Sikhs taking pride in their common cultural identity. Dialects like Mirpuri and Poonchi are akin to Gojri, Dogri and Punjabi. Common cultural markers should be emphasized and the mass media can become the best tool to do so. Nothing can surpass the collective strength of a secular linguistic and cultural identity to provide resistance against the religious appeal of militancy in the Muslim-dominated districts. Unlike the Kashmir valley, which is separated from Pakistan-administered Jammu and Kashmir by high mountains and linguistic barrier the reality in Jammu is the opposite. The radio and television of the state-controlled Pakistan media has a strong reception in this part, and it relays programmes in the same languages spoken on this side. This is quite distinct from the poor quality of reception that the Indian state-controlled Doordarshan often provides to the hilly parts of the district. Similarly, in the plains, along the international border, programmes made in Jammu city are popular in Punjab province in Pakistan and a few individual artists from Jammu even receive fan mail from across the border. Special funds allotted by the central government for items such as the full-fledged Kashir channel fails to meet the specific needs of the people of either of the two regions.[4] Broadly speaking, there are two distinct families of languages. One is known as Kashir, as Kashmiri is locally called, and the other family includes languages and dialects such as Dogri, Punjabi, Gojri and Pahari. There should be separate channels producing and telecasting in the two families of languages. The latter are relevant to the Jammu region as well as to Pakistan-administered Jammu and Kashmir and Punjab province in Pakistan. The Kashir channel, as it exists today, is an admixture of different families of languages that does great injustice to the Kashmir valley, and is a source of humiliation to Jammu region. TV and Radio Stations, which are geographically and ethnically closer to the area, must be upgraded for production and telecast or broadcast services. Even from the economic perspective this would be a cheaper remedy, as airing programmes from the Valley to the rest of the state requires the use of satellites and other sophisticated equipment. Jammu's cultural icons of yesteryears like Malika Pukhraj, Allah Rakha and K.L. Sehgal, and literary stars like Krishna Chander and Chirag Hasan Hasrat are binding forces for all the communities in the area. Their memories need to be kept alive and their contributions celebrated.

The Economic Component

Different parts of Jammu have their own economic problems. Rajouri and Poonch for instance, suffer from lack of economic infrastructure. The main livelihood in this area used to be from recruitment to the state or British Indian armies. During the post-independence era, the rate of recruitment was reduced drastically. Due to the rocky and infertile terrain and no past experience of other trades, there were no alternate occupations available to the people of this region. Being at the remote edge of the country, it also nurses grievances of economic neglect since 1947. The border districts were on the historic Mughal road to the Kashmir valley. They were also economically and socially integrated with prosperous cities like Rawalpindi and Lahore in Punjab province in Pakistan. But the scenario changed and these districts became isolated. Poonch district is now 225 kilometres from the nearest railhead, that is Jammu city.

Once famous for tourist attractions, successive governments turned a blind eye to its problems. Bearing in mind these facts, the security forces can launch special recruitment drives to provide employment in these border districts. This will go a long way in creating defence infrastructure in the form of manpower that has a martial tradition and knows the local terrain. If this happens, even the efficiency of the forces belonging to Punjab and the neighbouring parts of the country will improve due to the similarity in language. Special funds for developing the road infrastructure should be provided. Subsidized air taxis must be started for emergency movements that could also become a commercial proposition. As long-term steps for improving the industrial base of the belt cannot be taken at the current time, owing to the unsuitable environment prevailing, emphasis must be put on short-term measures. Traditional occupations such as sericulture, cottage industries, apiculture, horticulture and resin extractions for turpine need to be encouraged.

Doda district in Jammu suffers from similar economic problems. Most of the recruitment to the militants' ranks occurred in the rural parts of the district. Ameliorating the problems of the population of Doda district has received lowest priority by successive governments. For instance, the Bhaderwah-Bani or Bhaderwah-Chamba road network could have provided the district direct access to the rest of the country, thus opening the doors for socio-economic development and tourism. There are several villages even within the district that are still not connected by road. Doda is one of the districts in the state where even government officials have to walk for hours to reach their official destinations.

Kishtwar is a large district and even within it there are economic disparities. Some of the areas of the district like Wadwan and Dachin can only be accessible after walking for days. In these areas the militants operate freely as there is also a lack of security checks. Locals allege that the police do not patrol the remote areas thus creating an environment of insecurity. The absence of a proper road network also affects the security forces in their attempts to overpower militants. Kishtwar needs a specific package to ensure road connectivity. The district has natural provisions for power generation and the authorities have shown some interest in this. It can become an energy surplus district, exporting energy to the rest of the state or even outside. This would open the floodgates of economic development, providing employment to a large number of currently unemployed youth.

One of the chief reasons for joining militants in the district was the low economic level of the people, with a considerable number living below the poverty line. Construction of some dams for hydel power, such as Dul Hasti in Kishtwar and Baglihar in Chanderkote on the river Chenab have been started, but in both projects the local labour force has been inadequately employed and employers are accused of inhuman treatment by the local workers. Several agitations have taken place in these areas as a result, thus further increasing the unrest of the local people. In the hilly tracts of Reasi and Kathua districts, road connectivity is once again, poor. The weak transport and communication networks in these hills act as an obstacle to the smooth movement of security forces particularly in the upper reaches of the Gool-Gulab Garh area of Reasi district. In the plains of Jammu, a series of terrorist attacks have resulted in de-industrialization, with several national-level organizations leaving the region and shifting to other areas of the country. An anti-terror insurance cover should be provided to industrialists so that it acts as an incentive for them to invest in the region.

The Political Component

Lack of political share in the decision-making process relating to the problems of Jammu since independence is the main cause for its backwardness and the failure to fulfill its aspirations. Political power in the post-independence era is centralized in the leadership based in Srinagar. There have been various regional agitations to end Kashmir's hegemony over Jammu. For instance, there was the famous Poonch agitation in 1978 in which it was alleged that the state government led by Sheikh Abdullah (from Kashmir) was responsible for nepotism in recruitment to government jobs. The agitation started on a minor issue but snowballed into a movement, which engulfed the entire Jammu region. Both Muslims and Hindus jointly participated in the agitation against what they termed as 'Kashmiri domination over Jammu'.

However, some leaders of the same movement allege that an extremist group of Hindus compromised with the Kashmiri leadership and sabotaged the popular agitation, thus sowing the seeds of Hindu-Muslim discord. The people's frustration in the region in the absence of secular outlets has often led to communal articulation. The last decade has seen attempts to break regional identity, and this has contributed to the militancy in the region. The damage to regional identity has been at the cost of communal harmony in the area. In 1998, the National Conference government officially sponsored a move in this regard in the form of a report that recommended the division of the region into three areas, largely based on communal lines. The traditional links between the people of the region were sought to be broken under the guise of economic considerations. To the general disaffection with the politics of the state has recently been added the demand of statehood for Jammu. The Rashtriya Swayamsevak Sangh (RSS) started this move after its Kurukshetra Resolution in June 2002. An RSS-sponsored group, the Jammu State Morcha, also took part in the assembly elections. In the Muslim-dominated border belt, this demand is seen as an attempt to enforce Hindu domination. In a fierce reaction to the statehood demand there has been another counter movement by the Muslim belt for separate regions of their own, named Pir Panjal in the Rajouri-Poonch districts and Chenab valley in Doda district.

To summarize, the political scene tended to polarize the Hindus and Muslims, each fearing the domination of the other. The move to trifurcate the state has led to demands to trifurcate Jammu, based purely on communal lines. This political development has resulted in a trend to reduce the resistance of the people against jehadi militants who seek support on religious consideration. One of the main planks of the anti-militancy strategy should be the strengthening of Hindu-Muslim relations and encouraging a common leadership of the two communities, as also secular politics. Counterterror strategies in Jammu must start with rooting out the factors that were responsible for the outbreak of militancy in the first place. The mass killings of Hindus were often defended as acts of reprisal against those by Hindu extremists. Even the victims of some of the gruesome massacres corroborate this theory. For instance Shubh Sharma, who lost his entire family in the infamous Champnari massacre of Doda district in which 28 members of a bridal party were killed, provided some revealing inputs.[5] According to the boy, his family members were killed in retaliation for the killing of four Muslims by RSS workers who had drowned them in the river Chenab in the nearby area. Following that incident, militants issued a warning to the villagers not to celebrate any marriage in the village. For quite some time the warning had its impact and no one dared to violate it.

However, the militants got it wrong when they attacked a bridal party belonging to another village. Immediately after the incident there was a huge communal upsurge in the entire region, particularly near the district headquarters, i.e. Doda town. Hindus started migrating so that they lived together and the Muslims did the same with their co-religionists, leaving a communal imprint on the social fabric. As Shubh says in frustration, 'We (Hindus and Muslims) live in two different worlds now.' The political environment in the region further worsened the communal relations in the area. Political parties exploited the insecurities of both Hindus and Muslims. While the support of the Muslims for the militants increased, the Hindu reaction was represented by parties like the BJP, which added fuel to the fire with its shrill voices demanding the handing over of the district to the army. As discussed earlier, when the Disturbed Area Act was clamped on the region, the entire region was handed over to the army, and it undermined the role of the civil administration, thus facilitating the task of the militants.

No counter-terror strategy can escape the fact that the region's communally-sensitive precepts need to be sensitively tackled. Society as a whole cannot fight terror if we exclude any section of it. Muslims in mixed areas saw VDCs as an attempt to place them in an insecure environment, as recruitment of Muslims to the VDCs is negligible. Though the threat perception to the Muslims from the militants is less, there are numerous Muslims who want protection from them – for example members of the mainstream parties, who have in the past borne the brunt of militant attacks. There is also a need to keep a check on the VDCs to ensure that they consist of both communities to prevent Muslim feelings of insecurity.

On the social level the efforts of non-government organizations need to be promoted as they provide a social platform for Hindus and Muslims to come together and collectively work for the upliftment of the district. This can be substantiated by the efforts of Gandhian organizations that are working in Doda. The traditional bonds between the Hindus and Muslims must be restored. Greater responsibility lies on community leaders who should encourage communal harmony. In areas where militancy is at present at its peak, non-fulfilment of the aspirations of the people has often been cited as reason for people becoming disillusioned with the political mainstream. Unlike the Kashmir valley, in Jammu, we cannot blame unfair elections as the main cause of popular alienation. However, disappointment with the lack of political say in the affairs of the state was apparent. There have been several political agitations in the region, which were eclipsed by the larger Kashmir problem. The central and state governments continue to ignore the political aspirations of the people, and this is a factor in precipitating the deterioration of the security scenario in the region.

Piecemeal and Ad Hoc Measures

Piecemeal and ad hoc measures to appease communal and ethnic urges, without structural changes, only misfired. For instance, the Scheduled Tribes enjoy the benefits of political reservation in the legislature and in government services in other parts of the country, as enshrined in the Indian Constitution. But due to its special status, under Article 370 of the Constitution, and its own Constitution, Jammu and Kashmir does not have a similar provision for the Scheduled Tribes in the state. Thus Gujjars, one of the most important communities in the state, are deprived of this benefit, giving rise to a sense of disaffection. Similarly, the Pahari community started a movement for granting them Scheduled Tribe status, which every political party promises to give during the elections. The failure of the political parties to keep their promises to the community has left them frustrated.

If Paharis do not fit into the literal definition of tribals under the Constitution, constitutional safeguards could be evolved for them.

That militancy started in Kashmir and then gradually spread to Jammu is well known. In both regions, the source of arms, and later manpower, for militant activities are based in Pakistan-administered Jammu and Kashmir. Much scholarly and journalistic work has been carried out on the causes of the origin of militancy in the state. But the fact that it took several years to spread in different parts of Jammu, and declined much earlier than in Kashmir, points to significant peculiarities of its own, has somehow been overlooked. Jammu differs from Kashmir valley in several ways. The major languages spoken in Jammu belong to the same family while it is quite distinct from the language of the valley. Geographically, the valley is a vast plateau surrounded by lofty mountain ranges while Jammu is mostly hilly area. Politically, Kashmir has nursed grievances against the central government, which for want of adequate avenues of outlet, is supposed, eventually to have a violent outlet. Jammu's grievances, on the other hand, were mostly directed against the Kashmir-based political leadership under a centralized, constitutional and political system. In the absence of an adequate secular outlet, regional discontent tends to get a communal one. Communalism was further encouraged by the militant movement, which tried to represent one community and threatened the other, thereby aggravating communal tensions further. Knowledge of the geo-cultural background of the region, which is vital in order to be able to study the problem, has been provided in the first chapter. Further variations have been taken into account by micro-studies of different parts of the region.

The fact that Jammu is ethnically much closer to Pakistan-administered Jammu and Kashmir than both are to the Kashmir valley is of crucial significance to the study of the causes and character of militancy and its composition. When the stock of Kashmiri militants declined and non-Kashmiri militants were unwelcome in Kashmir valley, the so-called foreign militants were found to be more acceptable to the Muslims of Jammu. Events in the last six decades have indicated that a stable and harmonious state of Jammu and Kashmir cannot be formed without taking into account all the peculiarities of the region – geographic, administrative, cultural, economic and political. Security, it is now universally recognized, is not merely a job for security forces. It needs to be supplemented by political, social, cultural, administrative and constitutional means, which are pre-requisites for a harmonious society. This study of the rise and decline of militancy in the Jammu region, with its own peculiarities, is a contribution to anti-militancy strategies elsewhere.

Notes

1. After the opening of the Srinagar-Muzaffarabad road, four more LoC points were opened for transfer of relief material for the earthquake on October 8, 2005. Thereafter, the same number of points were opened for civilian traffic, including Chakan da Bagh and Tattapani to the south of the Pir Panjal where the maximum number of divided families live in the state of Jammu and Kashmir. Haji Pir pass in the Uri area of Baramulla district and Teetwal-Nauseri road in Kupwara district were the other LoC points opened to the north of the Pir Panjal in the Kashmir region. Later, similar to the Srinagar-Muzaffarabad bus service, the Chakan da Bagh-Rawalakot bus service was started on June 21, 2006.
2. The Srinagar-Muzaffarabad road was opened on April 7, 2005 as part of Confidence-Building Measures between India and Pakistan.
3. Front-page story: 'SHRC Office Locked in Jammu' in *The Kashmir Times*, December 6, 2007.
4. When it started, an annual budget of Rs.100 crores was earmarked for the Kashir channel.
5. Interview with Shubh Sharma.

Bibliography

Aash, Mohan Lal, *Cultural History of Doda, J&K* (Neesha Publishers: Jammu, 1991).

Abdullah, Farooq, *My Dismissal* (Vikas Publishing House: New Delhi, 1985).

Bloeria, S. S., *Pakistan's Insurgency vs. India's Security* (Manas: New Delhi, 2000).

Das, Durga (ed.), *Sardar Patel's Correspondence*, Vol. 1 (Navjivan: Ahmedabad, 1971).

J&K Information Department, *Jammu and Kashmir District Profile* (1998).

Hasan Khalid, *Memory Lane to Jammu* (Sang-e-Meel Publications: Lahore, 2003).

Lamb, Alistair. *Kashmir: A Disputed Legacy, 1946-1990* (Roxford Books: Hertfordshire, 1991).

Madhok, Balraj, *Jammu, Kashmir and Ladakh: Problem and Solution* (New Delhi, 1987).

Mahajan, Mehar Chand, *Looking Back* (Asia, 1963).

Phadnis, Urmila, *Towards Integration of Indian States* (Asia, 1968).

Puri, Balraj, *Jammu & Kashmir: Triumph and Tragedy of Indian Federalism* (Asia Book Corp, 1981).

————, *Simmering Valcano: Jammu's Relations with Kashmir* (Sterling, 1983).

———, *Jammu: A Clue to the Kashmir Tangle* (New Delhi, 1966).

———, (ed.), *Kashmir Affairs*, Bimonthly, 12 Issues (Delhi, 1959-61).

———, *Kashmir: Insurgency and After* (Orient Longman, 2008).

———, *Kashmir: Towards Insurgency*, *Tracts for the Times* (Orient Longman, 1993).

———, *Regional Autonomy in J&K* (Jay Kay Publishers, 1999).

Sahni, Sati, *Kashmir Underground* (Har-Anand,1999).

Saraf, M.Y., *Kashmir Fights for Freedom*, 2 Vols. (Lahore, 1978-79).

Schofield, Victoria, *Kashmir in the Crossfire* (I.B.Tauris, 1996).

Singh, Karan, *An Autobiography (1931-67),* (OUP: Delhi, 1981).

Vaid, S.P., *How Partition Rocked Jammu and Kashmir* (Shyama: Jammu, 2002).

Wali, Mohammad Aseer Kistwari, *A Scenario of Doda District* (Yasin Golden Publishing House: Doda).

Weiner, Myron (ed.), *State Politics in India* (Princeton University Press: Princeton, New Jersey, 1968).

Index

Abdul Qayoom Khan, 46
Abdullah, Farooq, 20, 49-50, 112
Abdullah, Mohammad, 85, 87, 97
Abdullah, Sheikh, 16, 19-20, 30, 116
Accession to alienation, 19-20
Ad hoc measures, 109-11
Al-Badr militant, 58
Al-Fateh militant outfit, 33
Alienation, 19-20, 47, 109
Alienation in Poonch, 47
Allah Rakha, 103
Amanullah Khan, 21, 23
Anti-terror strategy, 101-03
Arc of militancy, 25
Attacks in Doda, 31
Avtar Singh, 81
Azad Kashmir, 25, 37

Barshalla, 35
Bhaderwahi, 19, 30
Bimber Gali pass, 54
Bloeria, S. S., 46, 112

Chakan da Bagh and Tattapani, 96, 111
Champnari massacre, 35, 107
Character of militancy, 11, 26, 34, 44, 83, 110
Chowdhary, Ghulam Abbas, 16
Chowdhary, Mohammad Shaffee, 16
Chowdhary, Shabir, 25
Civil administration, 91, 99-101, 108
Communal, 11, 18, 30, 34, 36, 47, 59, 78, 88, 92, 97, 106, 108-09
Communal killings, 26, 31, 34, 51
Communal riots, 15-16
Congress Party, 16, 20, 92-93
Counter-militancy operations, 11, 13, 92
Counter-terror strategies, 10, 89-92, 98, 107
Cultural component, 101-03
Cultural policing, 33, 60

Diversities, 19
Doda, 6, 12, 14, 22, 25, 27-38, 43, 46, 53, 56, 64, 69-70, 73, 80, 87, 92, 101, 104, 109
  militant groups, 31-32
  official view of militancy, 33-34
  political vacuum, 34-36, 47
  rise of militancy, 27-30
Dogra communites, 69
Dogra culture, 27
Dogri, 19, 77, 102

Economic component, 103-05

Firdous baba, 31-32, 37
Foreign militants, 42, 51, 111

Gaddis, 32, 62
Gandhi, Rajiv, 20, 23
Geo-ethnic variations, 26-27
Ghulam Nabi Azad, 12, 23, 92
Gojri, 19, 44, 64, 77, 92, 102, 103
Gujjar community in militancy, 67
Gujjars, 14, 25, 44-45, 48-50, 56, 61-62, 65, 67, 72, 75-76, 109
Gujjars and bakerwals, 44, 61, 76

Haji Buland Khan, 66
Harkat-ul-Ansar, 25
Harkat-ul-Mujahideen, 25, 33
Highway routes, 62-76, 98
Hindu community, 16, 31, 70
Hindu-Muslim relations, 107
Hindus, 15-16, 18, 26, 33, 35-36, 54, 57, 60, 62, 65, 67, 74, 78, 87-88, 93, 97, 101, 108
Hindus and Muslims, 31, 47, 72, 78, 87-88, 101, 107-08
Hizbul Mujahideen, 21, 23, 25, 27, 32, 65, 90
Human Rights Commission, 98
Human rights institutions, 98-99

Indo-Pakistan wars, 16-18, 46
Infiltration routes, 24, 70, 81, 91
Infiltrators, 24, 37, 46, 53, 70, 81
Initiation of militancy, 27, 39-61
  in Doda, 27
Intra-Militant rivalries, 49-50

Jaish-e-Mohammad, 21, 59
Jammu and Kashmir, 7, 9, 12, 14
  aftermath of the Indo-Pakistan Wars, 17-18
  diversities, 18-19
  from accession to alienation, 19-20
  Pakistan-administered, 11, 14-15, 32, 39, 52-53, 61, 78, 96-97, 101, 103, 110
  pre-partition profile, 13-15
  social scenario, 17
  socio-political scene, 16-18
  start of militancy, 20-21
Jammu and Kashmir Liberation Front (JKLF), 21, 27, 31, 65
Jammu city, 22, 26, 31, 33, 58, 77-88, 99, 102, 104
  effects of militancy on society, 87-88
  major strikes, 82-83
  militancy, 81-82
  suicide attacks in the city, 83-86
Jammu region, 10, 12, 14-15, 18, 22, 24, 26-27, 30, 36, 77-78, 89-111
  counter-terror strategies, 10, 89-92, 98
  reduction of militancy, 92-93

Kaluchak, 22, 84, 86
Kaluchak suicide attack, 86
Kashmir Valley, 9-25, 30, 32-33, 36, 39, 46, 56, 64, 90, 109-10
Kashmiri militancy, 80
Kashmiri militants, 65, 73, 81, 111
Kashmiri nationalism, 11, 27, 34
Kashmiri Pandit community, 26, 80
Kashmiri speaking muslims, 62, 64, 72
Kashmiri-speaking militants, 24, 45, 86-87
Kathua, 14, 22, 25, 36, 62, 64, 69-76, 80-81, 105
  local population in militancy, 75
  militant incidents, 74-76
Khalistan Zindabad Force, 80
Kishtwar, 22, 28, 30, 33, 35, 37, 62, 87, 92, 101, 104
Krishna Chander, 103

Krishna Rao, K.V., 82-83

Ladakh, 12-14, 20, 32, 36
Lashkar-e-Toiba, 21, 32, 38, 86, 97
Line of Control (LoC), 12, 15, 42-43, 92-93, 95-97, 111
Long-term solution, 10, 97-98

Maharaja Hari Singh, 19, 39
Mahore, 25, 53, 56, 62, 64-65, 90
Major strikes in Jammu, 82-83
Malika Pukhraj, 103
Mass killings of Hindus, 26, 33, 68, 107
Migration, 15, 34, 37, 42-43, 52, 57-58, 68, 78
  across the line of control, 42-43
  from Rajouril, 57-58
Migration of Hindus, 34
Migration of Muslims, 15, 78
Militancy
  attacks in Doda, 31
  character, 11, 26, 34, 44, 83, 110
  growth of, 9-10, 15, 26, 90
  in Doda, 27-36, 62, 73
  in Jammu, 9-11, 27-28, 91
  in Jammu region, 22-23
  in Kashmir valley, 20-21
  in Kathua, 70-76
  in Poonch, 6, 43-52, 93
  in Rajouri, 56-61
  in the State, 13, 20-22, 26, 33, 68, 80, 83, 110
  in Udhampur, 69-70
  major strikes, 57, 82-86
  outbreak, 19, 24-37, 51, 93, 107
  phase, 21, 48, 89
  sociological reasons, 27-31
  start of militancy in the state, 20-22
Militancy strikes, 77-88,
Militant groups in Doda, 31-32
Militant movement, 10-11, 21, 27, 34, 48, 89, 92, 110
Militant ranks, 27, 50, 80
Militants and the local culture, 50-52
Militant attacks, 36, 67-68, 72
Militants attacking Hindus, 57
Militants' highway route, 62-76, 98
Mirza Abdul Rashid, 58
Mughal road, 39, 44, 52, 60, 103
Muhammad Shabir Sheikh, 49-50
Muslim community, 10, 25, 36, 51, 58-60, 70
Muslim Gujjar community, 75
Muslim Janbaaz, 25, 27, 31-32
Muslim Rajputs, 14, 17, 42, 48

National Conference, 16, 19, 23, 49, 106
Nomadic community, 14, 64

Official view of militancy, 33-34
Operation Sarp Vinash, 43, 92
  outbreak of militancy, 19, 24-37, 51, 93, 107

Pahari, 19, 44-45, 49-50, 56, 61, 77, 103, 109
Pahari militants, 49-50
Pan-Islamic movement, 91
Peace process, 93-97
Phase of militancy, 21, 48-89
Pir Panjal range, 9, 18, 30, 42, 61, 64, 96
Political component, 106-09
Political party, 19, 35, 47, 109
Political scenario, 16-17
Political Vacuum in Doda, 34-36
Poonch, 14, 17, 19, 22, 24-25, 36, 39, 42-52, 54, 90, 102, 107
  alienation in Poonch, 47
  delayed response to militancy, 45-47

ethnic profile, 44-45
intra-militant rivalries, 49-50
militants and the local culture, 50-52
political factors, 47-49
specifics of militancy, 43
Surankote a liberated zone, 43
Pre-Partition profile, 13-15

Rafiq Khan, 50
Raghunath Temple, 22, 84-85
Rajiv nagar attack, 22, 85, 87, 97
Rajouri, 17, 22, 24-25, 36, 40, 44, 49, 52-61, 64, 74, 80, 90-91, 101, 107
attacks on the Muslim community, 58-59
effect of militancy on society, 59-60
Rajouri's strategic location, 52-54
Ramban, 22, 29, 64
Reasi, 14, 22, 25, 45, 52-53, 56, 60, 64-69, 74, 76, 85, 105
attacks on Hindus, 67-69
Gujjars joined militancy, 67
importance of Mahore Tehsil, 65
personal rivalries, 66
spheres of militancy, 64-66
Reduction of militancy, 92-93
Religious diversities, 9, 10
Rise of militancy, 27-30

Samba, 22, 79, 81, 86
Sanjuwan Army Camp, 85
Sehgal, K.L., 103
Shere-e-Poonch, 47
Shivalaya temple, 85
Sikh Militancy and Jammu, 80-81
Sikh militants, 73, 80-81
Socio-political scene, 16-18
Srinagar-Muzaffarabad bus, 96, 111
Start of militancy, 20-21
Suicide attacks, 83-86
Surankote, 43, 49-51, 92

Tanda Army Camp, 85
Terrorism, 9-10, 89
Thakrain-Hor and Sarwan, 35
Thakur, Santosh, 34

Udhampur, 14, 22, 36, 60-70, 74

Village Defence Committee (VDC), 36-37, 55, 58, 67, 69-70, 73, 108

Wali Mohammed Itoo, 82